MOSES

*A Short Account of the Life of
Reverend Moses Margoliouth*

Peter Jones

MINERVA PRESS

LONDON
MIAMI DELHI SYDNEY

MOSES: *A Short Account of the Life of Reverend Moses Margoliouth*
Copyright © Peter Jones 1999

ISBN 0 75410 728 0

First Published 1999 by
MINERVA PRESS
315–317 Regent Street
London W1R 7YB

Printed in Great Britain for Minerva Press

MOSES
A Short Account of the Life of
Reverend Moses Margoliouth

This book is dedicated to my mother,
and in memory of my father

Acknowledgements

I would like to express thanks to Minerva Press for their encouragement, right from the first communication they sent to me; I am so grateful too for their subsequent expertise. I owe special thanks to my cousin Philip Williams and his wife Joyce for their careful research and help with the text. I am particularly indebted to three people without whom this story would never have been completed. Firstly Miss Patricia Bell, archivist, of Bedford, whose knowledge of the history of her county and town is considerable; amongst her authorship is a most interesting study of the Jews in Bedford which has shed much light on the origins of some of Moses' friends. Secondly, Dr A.P. Joseph, interestingly a kinsman of the Revd Henry Joseph who baptised Moses Margoliouth. Dr Joseph is Chairman of the Birmingham Branch of the Jewish Historical Society of England, and has been so kind and patient in replying to my queries; he has allowed me to take advantage of his seemingly unlimited store of knowledge. Thirdly, Dr Marlene Silverman of Washington, DC, who is editor of the *Landsmen* the quarterly publication of the 'Suwalk-Lomza Interest Group' in America, which is concerned with the history and genealogy of Jewish families from the Suwalki and Lomza regions of Poland. She has been a fund of information about much of Moses' background, and in particular, her discoveries of the Goldberg family in France have uncovered for me secrets of the Margoliouth in-laws which would otherwise have remained hidden behind the curtains of 3 Rue de Birague. Her untiring work on the archives of Suwalki and Lomza is widely known and I hope sufficiently appreciated.

Others who have given me so generously of their time and knowledge: Gerard Abramovici, architect, of Paris, for providing Goldberg documentation and pictures of the Rue de Birague; Louis Armigues, Directeur des Archives et de la Documentation at the Ministère des Affaires Etrangères in Paris; Lucy Cuthbertson, of the Library and Information Services of the Foreign and Commonwealth Office; Radek Sikorski of Poland, author of *The Polish House*; Martin F. McGann, archivist, US National Archives, College Park, Maryland; Richard A. Cooper of The Jewish Genealogical Society of Great Britain; Dr Glen Cavaliero of Cambridge; Kate de Kersauson of the Louvre Museum, Paris; Richard Radford of the C. of E. Pensions Board; Caroline Picco and staff of the Chester Record Office; Dr Nancy Ball, historian, of Nantwich; Mrs Waltraud Field of Nantwich, for German translations; Mrs. Black of the Birkenhead Library; Angus Varley and staff of the Nantwich Library; Mark Priddey, archivist, Oxford; Hugh Hanley, County Archivist, Buckinghamshire Record Office, Aylesbury; Nina Evans of The British Library; Capt. David Jones, Ship's Captain, for advice on the Avenger disaster; Peter Chapman of the Grimsby Evening Telegraph; Alan Akeroyd, archivist, Huntingdon; Revd Walter King, Rural Dean of Huntingdon; John G. Durnall of Stockport; Brian Smith of Burnley; Tom Bradshaw of North Crawley, Newport Pagnell; Gerald R. Stratton of Newport Pagnell; Colin S. Mickleburgh, J.P. of Atherton, Manchester; Barry D. Bate of Christleton, Chester; Roy Willis of Mouldsworth, Chester; Florence L. Kershaw of Todmorden; Clemens Wachter, Archivist, University of Erlangen-Nuremberg; Martin Sixsmith, formerly of the BBC

Moscow; Frances Miller, archivist, Reading University; Glenda Waddell of Holy Trinity Brompton/St Paul's Onslow Square; Janet Smith, archivist, Chelmsford; Norman Scarfe of Woodbridge, author of *Innocent Espionage*; Adam Smith, Collections Manager, Braintree; Revd Dr Walter Riggans and Elizabeth Hockenhull of the C.M.J.; Revd S.R. Beckley, Vicar of St Catherine's, Tranmere; Karen Israelsen of Napier City Council, New Zealand; Editor of the Napier Telegraph, New Zealand; Bishop J.C. Duggan of Dublin; Revd Mark Gardner (Rector), and the Revd Margaret Gilbert of the parishes of Santry and Glasnevin with Finglas, Dublin; James P.J. Quinn of Hough, S. Cheshire, formerly of Dublin; Helen Field of Dublin; Tim Ashworth of the Salford Local History Library; Judith Baldry and Dora Rayson, archivists, Manchester; Dr Raymond Refaussé, archivist, Church of Ireland, Dublin; J. Wolfman, honorary archivist to the Jewish Community in Liverpool; Eileen Organ, archivist, Liverpool Record Office; Peggie Bowler (née Marston) of West Kirby; Candida Godber of Little Linford; Gill Paton, Haversham, near Little Linford; Revd Dr J.N. Morris of Westcott House, Cambridge; Sarah Schreiber of Stafford, Virginia, USA; James Knapp, London; Dr Brenda Hough of the Church of England Record Centre; Elizabeth Boardman, archivist, Oriel College, Oxford; Dr E.S. Leedham-Green, of the Cambridge University Library; and last, but by no means least, Gerald Hansard of Gisborne, New Zealand (see preface). I have received encouragement too from Lord Lindsay, whose ancestor Moses Margoliouth bumped into in Paris during the course of that exciting summer of 1847.

Moses Margoliouth once complained that his name had been 'thrown in the background'. It is unfortunate for him that fate has chosen an amateur to try to reverse this process; but perhaps, with the help of those named above, it can be said that he has emerged, to some degree at least, from the shadows of the past.

Preface

When the reader comes to the end of this book, which I hope he eventually will, he cannot think that it was appropriate for the parish of Wybunbury in the diocese of Chester, to be the centrepiece of this story. To Moses Margoliouth, his time there meant little. It must have seemed to him, in later life, to have been rather like the proverbial sparrow flying through a tiny room, through one window and almost immediately out at the other. But by an odd chance, the story does start there, and the events of his life radiate from that centre, extending at times to what would be considered by the standards of the time far-flung and exciting places.

Some time ago, I found at the back of a drawer a slim volume of sermons. The book was published in 1854 and the author was the Reverend Moses Margoliouth, 'curate of Wybunbury'.

Wybunbury was, up to the time of my father's tenure of the living (1946–1971), a large country parish in south Cheshire. To the north its boundaries extended to the edges of Crewe and Nantwich. The parish included many small townships and, to the south, it was almost running in to the bordering counties of Shropshire and Staffordshire.

Sadly, much has changed. The historic parish boundaries have been altered since those days. Inappropriate and undisciplined planning has transformed for ever the character of the village itself, and the ominous expansion of Crewe – always a threat since the early days of the railway system – is relentless in its menacing approach. But in the days of Moses Margoliouth this was in the future. It was then an unspoilt, idyllic landscape, and in writing of that time one can in one's imagination sweep away the scars of modern times and return to the more leisurely times of Queen Victoria. However, I was to discover that in many ways Moses was not a typical product of that tranquil scene; his horizons stretched way beyond the peaceful meadows of sleepy Cheshire, and his exotic and almost mysterious background was a world away from that of the average Brontë curate.

As I have said, I started off, and my curiosity was aroused, by this single unpretentious book. Interesting to me was the connection with Wybunbury, but the author also bore a name to excite unusual interest in anyone. A Jew perhaps? And yet a Christian. Where had he come from? What became of him? Did he die young, or live to pursue his career in the Anglican ministry? Was it possible to discover any answers to these questions? I was soon to find that an eventful and, at times, exciting life was about to be revealed.

The book itself was printed in Nantwich, by E.H. Griffiths, and was published in London by Longmans, then rejoicing under the extended and colourful name of Longman, Brown, Green, Longmans, and Seeleys. It was bound by Straker of Monkwell Street, London, as indicated by a small sticker on the inside cover. The reading matter is divided into four parts:

1. The Dedication.
2. The Introduction.
3. The Sermons.
4. A list of works by the same author.

I shall deal with each of these in turn and try to draw

conclusions from the clues therein.

1. He dedicated his book of sermons appropriately to his Vicar – the Revd James Hayes. The Revd Hayes had come to Wybunbury in 1817 as curate and, almost hard to believe, he was still curate twenty-six years later when his persistence was rewarded; in 1843 he was presented to the living and moved into the vicarage. He remained as Vicar until his death in 1858.[1] Certainly at the time he was writing his dedication, the two seem to have got on well together: 'Our relation,' says Moses, 'has hitherto proved a very happy one.' He goes on, 'Our views – whether on scriptural truths, or on ministerial or parochial work – seem in entire accordance.' Perhaps more significantly, he says, 'For myself, I feel grateful to the great Bishop of the church for appointing me, for a time at least, to labour in this portion of His worldwide vineyard.' So it would seem that Wybunbury's curate had no intention of ending his days in this sleepy part of Cheshire and emulating the achievement of his vicar. Moses also tells us of the exact date of his arrival in the parish – 'it is just twelve months to a day since I entered upon my labours here,' and as the dedication is dated 16th May, 1854, we know that he came to Wybunbury on that date in 1853.

2. In the introduction to the sermons, he explains that they were delivered in the presence of his vicar, 'in the Parish Church of Wybunbury in the solemn season of Lent just past.' And he adds, as a matter of local interest, that 'they are printed and published with a view of augmenting the building fund for the erection of a school which shall serve also as a place of worship, in a poor and very ig-

---

[1] He died 14th November, 1858, aged 68.

norant district in the above extensive parish.' This is known as the Stapeley Broad Lane School, which was indeed built and completed in 1854, and on the first Sunday of the month my father took a service of Holy Communion on its premises, in accordance with the aspiration of its foundation. Moses also goes on to say that he hopes 'the unpretending work' (i.e. the sermons) 'will produce in many a heart and soul GENUINE REPENTANCE, and cause them to experience the BLESSED EFFECTS emanating therefrom'. The capital letters are Moses' own.

3. The Sermons were, of course, the whole purpose of the book, and comprise nine Lenten addresses – the subject, the fourteenth chapter of the Book of the Prophet Hosea. They reflect on the disloyalty of the Children of Israel to their God, and he points out that their only hope of salvation is through repentance. Taking the Book of Hosea as a whole, this behaviour of the Israel-ites was a mirror-image of the life of the prophet himself. Hosea had a wife who had been unfaithful to him just as the Israelites had been unfaithful to God. Moses referred to chapter fourteen and the need for repentance as 'very important'. It took some time into my researches for the dramatic relevance of this passage to dawn upon me.

4. Lastly, at the end of the book, and occupying three pages, are matters under the heading 'Works by the same author'. Covering two pages of this is advertised as 'being ready for the press these three years', the Hebrew Old Testament, with 'critical, philological, historical, polemical and expository English comments.' There is an interesting list of subscribers, who had already each paid one guinea to reserve their copy, and this projected

work was to be in three volumes, each volume to comprise six hundred and fifty pages. He clearly at this time needed many more would-be purchasers and, sad to relate, this monumental work never came to fruition. It is interesting to note at this stage that Moses was later to say that he had spent nearly six thousand pounds on this endeavour which, brought up to date, would be well over two hundred and fifty thousand pounds in today's money.

We are also told that in 1853 he had delivered and published his farewell sermon at St Bartholomew's, Salford, so we know he came from there to Wybunbury. While at Salford he had earlier published a sermon entitled 'Holmfirth's Solemn Voice'; an address on behalf of 'the sufferers from the calamitous visitation at Holmfirth'.

An account of this disaster will be given later.

He had also published *An Exposition of the 53rd Chapter of Isaiah*, (1846), *A Pilgrimage to the Land of My Fathers,* (1850), *The History of the Jews in Great Britain,* (1851), and what was to be of special help to me at this stage, *The Fundamental Principles of Modern Judaism Investigated* (1843) as in this, his first book, he wrote as a preface, a short memoir which was to prove vital in discovering some of the details of his early life.

I am grateful to many people who have helped me gather information about the Revd Moses Margoliouth and a list will be found elsewhere of those who have so kindly and patiently replied to my questions and, where possible, sent me documentary evidence. I hope this list is complete. As mentioned I am especially indebted to Patricia Bell, Anthony Joseph and Marlene Silverman. I should particularly like to pay tribute to my cousin Philip Williams of Digswell in Hertfordshire. He and his wife soon caught my enthusiasm, and have spent hours and travelled miles in pursuit of details of Moses' life. I have received kind help also from the Hon. Mrs Richard Godber of Little Linford, Buckinghamshire, for reasons which will become apparent in due course. She holds the office of Churchwarden of the beautiful little church of Little Linford. But perhaps for me, the most unexpected discoveries throughout the course of my investigation came in response to a letter I sent to the Editor of the *Napier Telegraph*, New Zealand. Almost miraculously, this brought Gerald and Diana Hansard to my door, bringing information of which, at the start of my researches, I could scarcely have dreamed.

Within so short a time after his death, Moses Margoliouth was forgotten, and I hope the following pages telling of the varied and so often exciting events of an heroic life will interest the attention of the reader of this 'unpretending work'.

Peter Jones
August, 1999

The Vicarage, Wybunbury, 1847.
Original drawing in author's possession.

Contents

Chapter I
Early Years

The town of Suwalki in Poland is situated some one
hundred and twenty miles to the north-east of Warsaw,
near the Russian border, and Moses Margoliouth was born
there in 1815[1] of Jewish parents.

Tracing families, particularly Jewish emigrants from
Eastern Europe at this period, can be intriguing, difficult,
and at times impossible. Many such people would change
their names, in some cases taking on the name or names of
relatives already established in the West. Indeed it is worth
noting that although surnames were a legal requirement,
Jews at this time did not feel particularly attached to them.
For the purposes of this book, it is assumed that
Margoliouth was the family name in Suwalki – after all, it is
the name Moses assumed from 1837–8, and the name he
passed on to his children. But *overwhelming* evidence exists
which suggests that this was not his name in Poland, and
there are several clues which indicate that Moses' father's
name was Epstein, or Epszteyn. This name crops up in the
final stages of this story relative to Moses' nephew George –
see especially reference to the latter's listing in Venn's
Cambridge alumni, (see Appendix V) – although in the
1950s, *his* son Herschel stated that his father had *reverted* to
the name Margoliouth – not *adopted* the name on being
baptised in England by his uncle. However, much research

---

[1] Not in 1820 as was generally claimed in his lifetime.

into the records of Suwalki and district indicate that a family bearing the name Epstein fits into the other facts known about Moses, his parents and his various siblings. Taking this as being so, the mystery remains as to why he chose the name Margoliouth following his departure from Poland. The only reasonable answer seems to be that he assumed, probably on the occasion of his baptism, an ancestral name derived from one of his parents.

Regarding the evidence for Epstein, there are records of a Gershon Epstein, born in the last decade of the 18th century, (c. 1796–8) son of Jacob Epstein. This Gershon married Tauba, daughter of David Merecki (= Meretzki, a surname indicating that her family once lived in the Lithuanian town of Meretz), and of course if this assumption is accepted as correct, she was Moses' mother. This is, for all practical purposes, confirmed by Moses' English (Liverpool) baptismal certificate, where his mother's name is given as Toba, or Toby (the writing is poor) i.e. Tauba. In Poland there is a birth record for their son Joshua, 1819 (d. 1883), and also for Israel (Izrael), 1824, and these are two of his brothers' names mentioned by Moses in later correspondence from England. Nevertheless, and to avoid confusion, the family name used throughout this narrative will be Margoliouth.

Suwalki, the home of the Margoliouth/Epstein family was then a comparatively poor town, in a remote part of a windswept region, but since 1866 it has been the chief town of the province which also bears its name. It is an ancient settlement – in 1667 it was described as a 'large village' – and it received its town rights in 1715.

The origin of the name Suwalki is not known, but in early times that part of Poland – an area much larger than the province of today – was called Sudauen by the Germans, and in Latin was Terra Sudorum. In times of conflict the countryside was able to offer refuge with its lakes and forests, and Lithuanians in particular fled to its protection.

Polish history is particularly complicated. Suwalki was in a part of the country which came under Prussian rule at the Third Partition of 1795, but Napoleon Bonaparte was on the march, and his aggression was soon to dominate much of the continent. By the Treaty of Tilsit in 1807 that section of Poland was annexed to what had become a puppet of Napoleon, the Grand Duchy of Warsaw. After the retreat from Moscow, the Russians took over, a situation confirmed by the Congress of Vienna. During Moses' youth Poland was ruled by the Tzar of Russia, using the title King of Poland, allowing the country a degree of autonomy, but in 1831 the failure of a nationalist uprising led to Russian oppression, and all patriotic aspirations were suppressed.

In winter in those frosty lands, even today, wolves roam the nearby forests, and it is an area dangerously situated near the Russian border, which has always made Suwalki strategically vulnerable. To the north, within striking distance, lies the Baltic Sea, and from the coast there one can sail almost directly north to Stockholm. In the early nineteenth century the town struggled to support itself by means of local agriculture and timber from the forests. Now the economy is based on such industries as food processing, textile weaving and the manufacture of building materials. Nearby are numerous lakes and a national park, and it is one of the most environmentally clean regions of Poland, now becoming increasingly attractive to tourists. It was the birthplace, in 1907, of Abraham Stern, whose terrorist gang was responsible for many outrages in the thirties and forties, including the assassination of Lord Moyne in Cairo in 1944.

In the late eighteenth century, Jewish settlement started slowly and on a small scale. When the town achieved its freedom in 1715, the Kamadulan Order divided the land into parcels but for many years no Jews took up occupation. It is recorded that in 1808 only about forty-five Jews lived in the town, a very low figure compared with many other smaller towns in the area, but by 1827 this had risen to over a thousand. In the very early years of the nineteenth century the town enjoyed little economic development, and this must have reflected on the Jewish community. Things gradually changed, however, and with growth in numbers came a slow increase in wealth. Suwalki suffered much in the 1830–31 uprising, but Moses' family seems not to have done so, and throughout the 1820s and 30s the Margoliouths slowly came to share in this advancing prosperity. Moses' father, Gershon (George) Margoliouth was a merchant and shopkeeper in Suwalki – an important man and well respected by his fellow townsfolk – and as a husband and head of a growing family, he had achieved position and affluence in the town. It was a time when the situation of Jews in the community was particularly favourable compared with elsewhere in Eastern Europe; Frederick the Great had removed many of their disabilities, and with Napoleonic influence, the Grand Duchy of Warsaw had been organised very much along French lines.

Moses was one of at least eleven children of the family; the names are known of three sisters: Szyfra (b. 1832),[2] Gitla (b. 1833)[3] and Merya (also b. 1833); there were seven or eight brothers of whom seven can be named: Moses himself, Isaiah, Israel, Joshua, Herschel, Chaim and Matys. The Margoliouth parents were devout, and their children were brought up in all the strict observances of their forefathers. They were a family of antiquity and distinction: both his parents were descended from families 'renowned

---

[2] Married Josiel Berkman.
[3] Married Josiel Gibianski.

in the annals of Spain'. It is speculation, but nevertheless likely, that earlier generations had fled from that country at the time of the Jewish expulsion in 1492, and some of Gershon's ancestors eventually found their way to Metz,[4] and Moses' father had often dreamed of visiting that city to ascertain the state of the Jewish nation there. Gershon particularly had in mind one of his notable forbears – Tobias Cohn, born in Metz in 1652, whose father had fled from Poland to Metz in 1648 to escape the Cossack revolution. After their father's death, Tobias and his brother returned to Poland in 1673, and Tobias, under the patronage of the Elector of Brandenburg, eventually graduated from the University of Padua as a doctor of medicine, in which profession he achieved considerable distinction. For some years he lived in Adrianople[5] where he served as medical adviser to five successive Sultans. He eventually died at Jerusalem in 1729.

Thus it is clear that Moses came from distinguished academic ancestry. He went to school at the age of four, and from an early age he showed a precocity and understanding beyond his years and which reflected the intelligence of his forebears. It was fortunate, too, that his parents well appreciated the gifts possessed by their clever child. He was naturally brought up from this tender age to believe that the New Testament was the work of the devil, and that it was wicked to give even the most cursory attention to the teachings of Christ. Moses, in later years, would often tell the story of his first encounter with the name Jesus and the consequent fury it evoked in his father. When first starting to read at school, when only four or five, he was studying one day the 24th Psalm in Hebrew: 'The Lord Strong and Mighty'. The Lord, Jehovah, and Strong,

---

[4] Then in Germany.
[5] Now Edirne.

Ezuz. It happens that the Hebrew Ezuz is the Polish pronunciation of Jesus, and when he was later telling his parents what he had been reading, his father thought the subject had been Jesus. He angrily told the child never to repeat the name as it defiled his lips. This remained in his memory and for many years he always felt uncomfortable when he came across the 24th Psalm. In his own copy of the Bible, he folded down the page on which it was printed.

When only six he was made to learn the six hundred and thirteen Precepts. The version he studied was the one by Rabbi Gedaliah of Amsterdam, published in 1745. During these years his father employed a private tutor to take care of his education until, in about 1824, he was sent to attend Rabbi Jacob's School in Preroshla, some ten miles away. There he studied the Talmud until, he said, 'I became a slave to it'. At the same time his father paid for him to have private instruction in Polish literature, and under the same supervision he also studied Russian and German; accomplishments which were to prove vital in the years ahead. A year later he went to school in Grodno, a substantial town some forty miles south east of Suwalki, just over the border. The school he attended there was presided over by Rabbi Chayim – 'a great and celebrated man.'

He went on to finish his rabbinical education at Kalvarija, a small town some thirty miles north of Suwalki, where he formed a close friendship with two fellow pupils which was to have influence on the momentous decision he was destined to reach just a few years hence. He and his friends would speak to each other in Hebrew, and the three of them would also make schoolboy attempts at composing Hebrew poetry. One day his two friends showed him a copy of the New Testament which the father of one of them had recently bought from a Christian missionary in

Konigsberg.[6] He started to read the book, again coming to the word Jesus, reminding him of the incident those years ago which had caused his father such displeasure. 'Away with that book,' he shouted, 'the destroyer of my peace.'

Soon after, he returned to full time study at home, and his parents ensured that every facility should be given to satisfy the enquiring mind of their clever son. He was the pride of his parents' heart, and no expense was spared. In return Moses repaid their generosity and satisfied their expectations by working hard and daily adding to his store of knowledge. He was concerned to receive at this time the disturbing news that his two schoolfriends from Kalvarija had succumbed to temptation and, as he put it, 'embraced infidel principles': they had become Christians. He also records that shortly after this time, whilst staying with relatives, he had access to the New Testament. He grasped the chance to read portions of St Luke's Gospel, mentally excusing himself on the grounds that he was checking the purity of the Hebrew. He was temporarily away from home and, while free of the constriction of his father's presence, he felt able, with some twinge of conscience, to indulge in this transitory and risky investigation. He was impressed, and seeds of unease were being sown – wonderings and doubts which he was quite unable to discuss with his parents back home. Were these chinks of light, he wondered, glimpses of the truth or temptations of the devil?

In 1833–4 he found himself uneasily caught up in a Jewish tradition which was to affect his life. Matchmaking was then the accepted method of choosing a partner, and Moses was unable to resist the pressure exerted on him by his parents. He faced the prospect with that same enthusiasm he had shown as a boy in learning the 613 Precepts. A suitable bride was found for him, no doubt satisfying his

---

[6] Then also in East Prussia and now called Kaliningrad.

parents' social and financial standards, and the arranged marriage took place with his family's blessing and approval. The chosen bride's name was Chaja Goldberg, and she came from Wladyslawow, not far from Kalvarija where Moses had attended school. Miss Goldberg was one of at least four children (she certainly had three brothers), and her parents were Ber and Rachel Goldberg. Although the status of the Goldbergs came up to the level demanded by Gershon and his wife, Chaja herself did not meet with Moses' approval. The traditional arrangement, which normally was reasonably successful, proved in this instance to be a disastrous one. Chaja remains a shadowy, malign figure in this story; at times pathetic, and at other times almost threatening. The marriage probably took place in 1834, in Wladyslawow and the following year Moses' wife gave birth to a daughter whom they called Miriam.

There is no doubt that Miriam was dear to her father's heart but, by this time, Moses was showing dissatisfaction and bitterness with the situation in which he found himself. With his keen intellect and, at this stage, suppressed ambition, he was no candidate for settling down in a remote, half-forgotten land. The trouble was, that for Suwalki, he knew too much. He had, in the long silent hours of his studies, visited in his imagination the more prosperous lands in the West, and siren whispers had echoed to him across Europe, from Spain, France, Italy and, no doubt from England too.

His marriage, forced upon him by the ancient usages of his nation, was a failure; but it is certain that this fact was hidden from the world beyond his immediate family. His wife, mysterious, does no more than momentarily flit across the stage in the course of this narrative. She takes no part in the story, yet is the very essence of the plot, and as the domestic problems grew more intense, Gershon took action. He decided to give his restless son a break: he would send him to France to cool his heels and hopefully, after a few months, Moses would return home refreshed, to resume the life which had been planned for him. Moses was, after all, the most intelligent of the family and the one most capable of reporting back from Metz on the state of things there. Margoliouth senior, tied down by his business in Suwalki, was anxious to find a deserving cause there on which he could bestow his philanthropy.

Moses had other ideas. In a mood of desperation he was ready to make a run for it; over the wall, a quick dash across open ground, and away to freedom. And so, towards the end of July 1837, after the drama and tension of saying farewell to his loved ones – his parents, his brothers and sisters, and his daughter Miriam, and one would assume that Chaja also was included in the ritual – Moses left home with, as he put it, 'the permission of my father'. This meant, of course, with Gershon's parental and, more vital, financial blessing. His exodus from Suwalki was not typical of the restless movement west which had already started, and was so soon to engulf every country in Western Europe and, momentously, the New World. His was a special case, and with all the speed he could muster he made for the large and busy port of Hamburg on the Baltic.[7] On arrival there, he decided, he would stop and sort out his next move. The main thing was that he had escaped from the claustrophobic atmosphere of Suwalki and had evaded, at least for a time, the miserable marriage which had been so cruelly imposed on him.

Once in Hamburg, arrangements, decisions, became twisted and confused; matters of conviction were soon to overcome those schemes which had been discussed in such detail round the dining table and chimney corner back

---

[7] It was largely from there that the great sailings to the New World took place, growing in pace as the century progressed.

home. He immediately learnt that, within three hours, a steam packet was due to leave for Hull; a port, he was told, on the east coast of England. He was further informed that it would reach its destination in just under forty-five hours. It was a spur of the moment choice – he would take it, and in doing so was about to seal his fate and change for ever his life and destiny.

★

In a moment of self-revelation, Moses was one day to describe himself as being short in stature and, as if to counterbalance this, he was confident, irrepressible, optimistic and possessed an attractive personality. He was ambitious but his ambition was tempered by a sense of humour, and he was undoubtedly very good company. Throughout his life he enjoyed many firm and long-term friendships. He was an extremely generous man, at times perhaps foolishly so and he, in turn, received kindness in good measure. He, of all his family, was best able to manage the inevitable language problems (he spoke at this stage not a word of English), and would face with relish the strangeness of life in a foreign country.

On arrival in England, for a little over two months, he toured the English countryside, enjoying to the full the strange panorama and the many sights and sounds which were all so new to him. He was utterly fascinated when, on 28th October his wanderings brought him to Liverpool where again fate was dramatically to alter the course of his life.

Liverpool at this time was one of the world's great ports, at the height of its prosperity, bursting with trade, cosmopolitan (ideal for Moses) and bubbling with optimism. It was the dawn of the Victorian age. Liverpool had already produced entrepreneurs like Sir William Brown, and it was here that families such as the Gladstones were making their mark and fortune. William Ewart Gladstone, nurtured in the very centre of the town, was twenty-eight, and would rise to occupy the highest office of state. Moses was overawed by his new surroundings and would one day, writing from the south of France, say that Marseilles 'could in no way compare with the splendid town of Liverpool'.

It was a place well used to coping with strangers, and amongst the charitable trusts established there for impecunious visitors was the Institute for Enquiring Jews, and Moses was indeed having to face the looming and inevitable problem of finance. The day of his arrival in town was a Friday, and that evening he met one J.G. Lazarus, a Christian Jew who was shortly to be appointed superintendent of the Institute, whose premises were situated on the corner of Fox Street and Beau Street. John Gladstone, William's father, was one of the trustees, and the Revd Henry Samuel Joseph,[8] an 'examiner'. This Institute was to provide accommodation for Moses and, at the same time, would offer him employment in the form of teaching – Moses, with his expertise in Hebrew, Russian and German was in reality quite a coup – and for him those long hours of study in Poland would reap a just reward. Mr Lazarus at once suggested he should read the New Testament, and Moses started on this task, only to find it an unsettling experience. He recorded that on the Monday (he had only been in Liverpool three days), his mind in a state of torment, he decided to leave and travel to London, there to request, and await, funds from his father which would enable him to return home to Suwalki. He reached Prescot, he says, and turning things over in his troubled mind, he suddenly decided to go back to Liverpool. It was evening time when he arrived, and he went straight to the house of

---

[8] See Appendix I.

Mr Lazarus and asked if he could borrow from him a copy of the New Testament in Hebrew. 'For three days,' he says, 'I did nothing else but read the New Testament, in which time I perused it from the beginning to the end.' He further recorded: 'A short time afterwards, the Lord in His infinite mercies enabled me to feel the efficacy of Christ's atonement.' He had become a Christian, and that chink of light which had caught the eye of a boy from Suwalki had become, for him, the Glorious Truth.

Through Mr Lazarus he came into contact with a number of people, including one who was to be especially helpful, and who became a close personal friend. This was the already mentioned Revd Henry Joseph, and he brought to bear on Moses much influence which was greatly to affect his future. Nathan Joseph (he changed his name later), was born a Jew in Bedford in 1799, the son of Michael Joseph, a silversmith. In 1811 he attended Bedford Grammar School for a year, and then in October 1812, was apprenticed by the Bedford Charity, for a fee of thirty pounds, to his father. Rather like Moses, he took an early interest in Christianity, but it was some years before, crucially, he came under the influence of the Revd T.S. Grimshawe, a keen member of the London Society for Promoting Christianity among Jews.[9] On 15th March, 1828, he was baptised by the Revd S. Sendall in St Gregory's, Lakenheath, Suffolk, taking on the name of Henry Samuel Joseph, as he was to be known for the rest of his life. He soon came to Liverpool, and in 1832 was living there in Great Nelson Street. In December 1836, he was ordained by the Bishop of Chester in St Peter's Church,

---

[9] Later the CMJ – the Church's Ministry among Jews and now known as the Church's ministry among Jewish people, with their headquarters in St Albans.

Liverpool,[10] and was immediately appointed to be Minister of St Simon's Episcopal Church in Gloucester Street, Liverpool. On 10th September, 1837, he baptised Samuel Levi Asher Herbert, his nephew, who became a close friend of Moses. Samuel was the son of John and Hannah Herbert, and Hannah was Henry Joseph's sister. Like Moses, Samuel was soon to be ordained, and became a correspondent of Moses during his travels in later years.[11]

On Good Friday, 13th April, 1838, Henry Joseph baptised Moses in St Simon's Church, Liverpool. The torment, the years of doubt and self-questioning, were over, and his future was to lie within the Church of England, whose liturgy and teaching were to be the guide of his life. But meanwhile, there were some immediate problems to be faced and overcome.

---

[10] Then in the Chester Diocese; the new Liverpool Diocese was formed in 1881.

[11] By which time Samuel Herbert was living in Sunderland. See also Appendix II.

Chapter II
Liverpool and Dublin

If his conversion brought joy and peace of mind, it did indeed also bring difficulties. His first duty was to tell his family back in Poland the painful news, and if he was hoping for a sympathetic response he was to be disappointed. 'The news,' Moses somewhat quaintly reported at the time, 'caused my father greatly to lament over my sorry condition.' This was the understatement of the year. His announcement was a terrible shock to his family, especially to his father, who was outraged. It acted like a depth charge, and Gershon at once instructed his wayward son to return home. Moses replied that his mind was made up, and in turn this led his father to say that he never wished to see his son again and all correspondence must cease. It was a family upheaval that neither side had sought nor anticipated.

However, Moses *did* continue to write and was greatly heartened by messages sent back to him by his younger brother Herschel who, whilst not approving, at least showed sympathy for his feelings. The rift was one of the penalties which Moses had to pay, at least for the time being. Happily it was by no means lifelong. Gershon did eventually show a generosity of spirit to an extent which was perhaps more than his son had a right to expect. A little later Moses wrote: 'These letters were no small trial to one who loves his parents above every earthly thing'. He continued to write to his 'dearest parents'.

The following is an extract from one of his brother's letters:

I must acknowledge that I do not find any unrighteousness in your letters but, at the same time, they are beyond my comprehension; therefore I know not what to do. I have resolved, by the help of God, to come to England, and to hear from your mouth more of your tenets, for I am very anxious about them.[1]

That the Lord may bless you, and be with you is the prayer of your affectionate brother,
Herschel

And later on, from his father:

My dear son,
I received your last letter, which revived my spirits; seeing, though I forbade you several times (in severe terms) to write to me any more, still you have persevered in writing; therefore I beg of you to pardon my past letters. And I assure you for the future, that as you were when at my house the dearest of all your brothers, and the beloved of my soul, and my heart and soul's chief desire was to make you a chosen vessel in the sight of God and men; with the same love and affection I love you still, and I will continue to do so until my life's end. I pray you not to be displeased with me for the past. Your ever affectionate father,
Gershon

These moving letters were bound to give him hope and comfort. Maybe one day some of his family would see the

---

[1] There is no evidence that Herschel ever visited England.

light, and in a determined spirit of optimism he prayed for their conversion too. His hopes on this point were to be realised for, some time later, (in 1843) he was able to write: 'I am thankful to the Hearer of prayer that my hope has been realised in some degree. Some of my very nearest and dearest have decidedly made up their minds to acknowledge Jesus as their Saviour and their God'. Poor Gershon must have wondered what the world was coming to.

Meanwhile, money was a problem, and for the time being Gershon was implacable. Moses records: 'My dear father, who never considered any expense too extravagant where learning could be got, would, in this instance turn a deaf ear, and moreover oppose it to the uttermost.' In the years ahead Gershon would bestow great generosity on his dearest son, but for the time being all funds from home were frozen and according to the house rules Moses could only stay at the Institute for three months. He was rescued from this predicament by a recommendation on his behalf to the Committee for the London Operative Jewish Institution – similar to the Liverpool foundation, but in the capital – and so, for the first time, he moved briefly to London where, thanks to his patient application back in Poland, he was able to continue to earn his living by teaching Hebrew and German.

He now came to see with increased clarity that his future lay in England. He was in straightened circumstances, but he could no more have sat morosely on a park bench, than return to Poland. The one course of action would have been an affront to his optimistic nature, and the other like returning to prison. Every day, in this new environment, he encountered fresh events and experiences which dazzled him, but at the same time he had to face the need to make ends meet and, equally vital, he knew he had to set about the task of learning the language of his adopted country. His friends and family back home in Suwalki were in his thoughts, but it was a time to concentrate on the stark realities of life, and he could only wait patiently for the Polish frosts to melt away in the east.

He kept in touch with Henry Joseph, and was soon back in Liverpool, where: 'I providentially met with some pupils' and for the time being this kept the wolf from the door. He had now firmly set his mind on being ordained into the Church of England so that he could, in his own words, 'devote myself entirely to labour in the Lord's vineyard'. This was to be the fulfilment of his dreams. He went on: 'The Lord in his mercy began then to pave the way for that step'. He also providentially met at this time an unnamed missionary who had just returned from India. He advised him on his immediate future; that is, to go to university. He also taught him Latin and Greek, 'in which languages I made considerable progress.'

University expenses were a major problem, but someone, again unnamed, came to his rescue. Someone of sufficient means, no doubt from Liverpool and enjoying the prosperity of the town, became his sponsor and patron. 'The Lord soon raised me up a dear friend, who assisted me in defraying my expenses on entering college.' One can speculate on the 'dear friend' but no evidence has appeared to point the finger. Was it Mr Lazarus, or the Revd Joseph?[2] Whoever, he was to enjoy the kindness of someone he knew well, but who was sufficiently unassuming and modest to insist on anonymity. It was an act of spectacular beneficence and, in January 1840, after due process of application, Moses obtained a place at Trinity College, Dublin. According to their records, he entered as a 'Schola Rabinica'; whether this was awarded for examined scholarship, or against a premium paid by his benefactor, is

---

[2] J.G. Lazarus possibly. Henry Joseph, unlikely. A strong candidate is Henry Leveaux, father of Edward Henry Levaux – see Appendix III.

uncertain. Whichever is the case, it is from Liverpool to Dublin that the action of the story is now transferred.

*

Amidst the silence of his studies, he occasionally must have allowed his mind to contemplate with amazement the course of his life so far. Here he was, a million miles from his religious and domestic background, studying for a degree at an English-speaking University. It was now 1840 and nearly three years since he had left his homeland. His conversion to Christianity needed no bolstering, but he now received heartening news that his two friends from Kalvarija, already committed Christians, had also been baptised – in Konigsberg, by the Christian missionary to the Jews there, Revd J.G. Bergfeldt. It is likely, too, that funds were starting to trickle through from his father; anguished, remorseful, yet proud of his adventuresome and academic son.

Trinity College, Dublin, widely known simply by the initials TCD, is a University of world renown and has been a centre of academia for centuries. It was founded under the patronage of Elizabeth I in 1592 as an Anglican institution, to be a 'counterblast to Popery', and to 'civilise' the Irish, and by tradition has been much used by English and Scottish Episcopalians. Over the past centuries it has expanded, and amongst its famous alumni have been Oliver Goldsmith, Edmund Burke and, more recently, Oscar Wilde. It possesses an important old library, built early in the eighteenth century, which houses one of the world's great treasures: the ninth century Book of Kells, a manuscript in Latin of the Four Gospels. It was in no way strange for a young man living in Liverpool to attend TCD, and it was perfect from Moses' point of view as it held special courses for students wishing to study theology and thence seek ordination.[3]

He was unfortunate to suffer two blows to his finances in his early days in Dublin. Just before his first college fees were due, he had his pocket picked, losing two ten pound notes, and almost at the same time he lost a purse, whilst browsing in a bookshop, with no less than twenty three sovereigns in it. It seems that he was being well provided for, and in spite of this considerable financial setback, he travelled to London for his first summer vacation, continuing his studies there under the tuition of Dr Alexander M'Caul (1799–1863), Principal of the Hebrew College, a Christian foundation.[4] Moses greatly admired Dr M'Caul and the pupil–teacher relationship grew into a firm friendship. There was good reason for this – not only was Dr M'Caul a graduate of TCD, he had also worked in Poland from 1821 to 1832 as a missionary under the auspices of the Society for Promoting Christianity among Jews. He had just been appointed to his post at the Hebrew College, and the following year became Professor of Hebrew and Rabbinical Literature at King's College, London. Although he was senior to Moses by some sixteen years they had similar interests, both academic and geographic. Dr M'Caul, more than most, appreciated the intellectual and spiritual ordeal of his pupil.

Whilst in London, Moses still kept in touch with the Joseph family, and on his way between Dublin and the capital he generally accepted their kind hospitality; they conveniently lived near Chester, at Rose Bank Cottage, Upton. It is significant that it was about this time that Henry Joseph was appointed to be representative of the

---

[3] A contemporary at TCD was Arthur Bell Nicholls, later to marry Charlotte Brontë. Mr Nicholls proudly showed his wife round the College on their honeymoon.

[4] Situated in the Palestine Square complex, Bethnal Green – then also headquarters of the CMJ.

CMJ in the north-west, based in Chester.

Moses, with his gregarious nature and intriguing European accent, was popular with his fellow students. He also began to mix in a circle of Dublin society which brought him in contact with a number of prominent people. Most crucially he met the Lindsay family of Glasnevin. The Rt Revd the Hon. Charles Dalrymple Lindsay, born in 1760, was in 1840 one of the most respected citizens of Dublin. Old, aristocratic, rich and holding high office in the Anglican Church, he was Bishop of Kildare and bore sway, somewhat remotely, over the diocese of that name. He occasionally occupied his imposing palace outside the city, but more often lived at his own private residence, Glasnevin House,[5] in the quiet and fashionable village of Glasnevin on the edge of Dublin itself. The importance of this connection on Moses' future career will soon become apparent.

During his time at TDC he produced three works of literary output which served to advance his reputation and at the same time gave him much personal satisfaction.

1.

In 1841 he translated, as part of his course, the Phoenissae of Euripides from Greek into Hebrew verse and it earned him much praise. He dedicated it to the Provost of the University.

2.

Moses greatly admired what is now termed the Establishment. He considered the English system of law, the political structure and the long-established class system to be exemplary. His high opinion of the Established

---

[5] Now housing the Convent of the Holy Faith. The Lindsay family later bought a smaller house nearby which they also called Glasnevin House.

Church was naturally unquestioned and he adored the Monarchy. He had arrived in England just four months after Victoria's accession and was in England at the time of the coronation in Westminster Abbey in June 1838. He was in Dublin in February 1840 when she married Albert, Prince of Saxe Coburg and Gotha in the Chapel Royal, St James's Palace. In due course Moses, with the rest of the nation, heard with joy of the birth, on 9th November, 1841, of Albert Edward, later Edward VII, and the royal baby was christened on 25th January, 1842. Even before the baptism had taken place, Moses had composed a poem in Hebrew to commemorate this happy event. He dedicated the poem to Prince Albert, and sent it to him under cover of the following letter:

To His Royal Highness PRINCE ALBERT

May it please Your Royal Highness to accept, from the hands of a Christian Jew, and an humble but devoted admirer of the Country in which Your Royal Highness holds so distinguished a station, a Hebrew Poem, composed by himself upon the introduction into the Christian Church by baptism of His Royal Highness the Prince of Wales. The poem was dedicated by feelings of admiration and gratitude towards the Country over which Her Most Gracious Majesty QUEEN VICTORIA sways with justice and mercy a righteous sceptre. That country in which the devoted servant of Her Most Gracious Majesty, and Your Royal Highness, was first led to know Him of Whom Moses and the Prophets did write, JESUS OF NAZARETH, THE KING OF THE JEWS.

The Poem will be found to contain a description of the National and Literary character of the English nation, and its August Queen, Your Royal Highness, the Coronation of Her Most Gracious Majesty, the auspicious Marriage of the Queen to your Royal Highness, the happy birth of a Princess and a Prince, and the Baptism of His Royal Highness the Prince of Wales.

The writer trusts that his humble endeavour will tend to strengthen in the breast of Your Royal Highness the interest already manifested towards the benighted children of the House of Israel.

I have the honour to subscribe myself,
Your Royal Highness' most humble and devoted servant.
MOSES MARGOLIOUTH
An undergraduate of Trinity College, Dublin.
Jan. 22nd 1842

Moses then records, 'I received a very kind acknowledgement of it from HRH Prince Albert. I sent a copy of the above-mentioned Poem to the Board of Trinity College, Dublin. They kindly deposited it in the College M.S. Library, and granted me a handsome prize for it.'

The TCD archives confirm that Moses was granted a 'premium' for this composition, and a copy is in the archives of the college library.

This last curiosity poignantly demonstrates his feelings, and serves to emphasise not only his loyalty to the Queen, but also his steadfast pride in being born a Jew. These sentiments remained as strong as ever throughout his life.

There was an interesting letter about this poem in the Cambridge Chronicle of 5th October, 1861. A correspondent who had recently returned from a tour of the continent had spent some time in Gotha, examining the ducal library there. He informed the paper's readers that the librarian had pointed out to him 'a manuscript Hebrew poem consisting of upwards of two hundred lines of exquisite penmanship, written on vellum, superbly bound in crimson velvet, and lined with amber satin'. He was informed that it was 'the production of an Anglo-Hebrew Christian muse'. Prince Albert, the librarian told him, had later arranged for it to be sent to his native place, where 'the sacred tongue is somewhat better understood than at Windsor'. Moses, many years later, gave a 'verbally literal' translation of the poem: 'Can there exist a spark of poetic fire in any man's soul, in this favoured land, and not be fanned into flame when, by the hearing of the ear, the joyful sound: *a son has been begotten to England's august Majesty*, has penetrated into such a man's soul? Praise to the Queen and Prince Albert – the latter doubly gifted in wisdom and excellence. Ye inhabitants of this isle, break forth into joy triumphant.' The poem also recorded, implying some miraculous infantile influence, that since the birth of the little prince, already two new Christian bishoprics had been formed, that of Jerusalem and Australia![6]

3.

In 1843 he published his first book, *The Fundamental Principles of Modern Judaism Investigated*. He arranged for it to be printed in Chester by T. Thomas, Eastgate Row, in the summer of 1843, having just graduated from TCD. He

---

[6] Susan Werner of the Forschungs und Landesbibliothek Gotha confirms that the poem is still safely in their possession. She writes: 'It appears that the poem you are searching for has survived and is in our library. It comprises 10 sheets of vellum, 27 x 18 cms, with 25 lines on each page. The cover is the original one and a label on the back page indicates that it was presented to the library by Prince Albert on 11th March 1858.' It is interesting that a note in the library index system states that the poem was written at Carlton Hill, Sydenham, Kent. It seems probable, therefore, that Moses spent Christmas 1841 in London, staying, perhaps, with his friend Alexander M'Caul. There is no other indication that he was away from Dublin at this time.

stayed with the Josephs while this matter was attended to. It was published in London by B. Wertheim, 13 Paternoster Row; in Chester by Evans and Ducker; and in Dublin by William Curry Jnr and Co. It was dedicated to his friend and mentor, Dr M'Caul.

It was an open criticism of what he called 'Modern Judaism', with arguments, in contrast, in favour of the veracity of the New Testament. He accused the Jews of idolatry or, as he put it, 'Jewish Popery', quoting as an example the absurdity of the 613 Precepts which he had been forced to learn as a child. In this same year, 1843, he wrote of his book: 'May the Lord of His infinite mercy grant that this my humble endeavour may tend to enlighten many of my poor brethren who are still wandering in the darkness of sin and error!'

Throughout his life, the pride he felt in his birth and ancestry was combined with a burning desire that his 'dear Jewish brethren' (for such they always remained to him) should share in that enlightenment which had befallen him. In a rare moment of bitterness he wrote, 'I must not expect anything from my unbelieving brethren but hatred and calumny'; he did many times cross swords with his fellow Jews, but more typically, 'I purpose briefly to show, with the help of God, that Jesus Christ, the Son of God, is the Prophet like unto Moses, and that God's mercy endureth for ever. I am not ignorant that this prophecy has been misconstrued by our Rabbies as referring to Elijah, Jeremiah, and other prophets; but I am also aware that it was only done in order to evade the irresistible Christian arguments on that point.'

He was not uncritical of his tuition at TCD. He felt that Hebrew should feature in the syllabus to a greater degree: 'I have met,' he says, 'many clergymen who lamented that there was too little attention paid in the Universities (and he was including his own) 'to Hebrew literature, and that most of the academic time is occupied comparatively in non-essential acquirements'. This was quite a bold observation to make at the time.

Just before graduating, he wrote, 'This being my last academic year, I trust, with the blessing of God, that I shall shortly be admitted into Holy Orders as a Deacon of the Venerable and Apostolic Church of England.'

So, his goal was in his sights. He had graduated from TCD, he completed his farewells in Dublin, and he now returned to his beloved Liverpool where he could resume contact with such as the Josephs, and Edward and Sarah Leveaux. It was amidst this euphoria that there now occurred in his life a sensational development: his in-laws, the Goldberg family, had moved from Poland to Germany and were then living in Berlin, where Moses' father-in-law was doing his best to earn his living as a writer. It was from there that Moses' wife, Chaja, and his daughter, Miriam, set out to join him in England.

His feelings on their arrival are not known, and are difficult to guess. Of course it is easily possible that this was the intended plan from the start – 'I will join you when the time is right.' But whatever is the truth, Gershon must have been the grand puppeteer pulling the strings and financially paving the way for their fresh start together. And so again, the shadowy, ephemeral figure of Mrs Moses Margoliouth is on the edge of the stage and Moses himself, in the centre, is again leading the life of a husband and family man. Above all, his little daughter Miriam has returned to him.

This is the dramatic background to those months which were leading up to his ordination. He again, through the good offices of his friend Mr Lazarus, temporarily earned his living teaching languages in the Institute for Enquiring Jews, and with his family set up home at 5 Juvenal Street, in the town.

About this time, towards end of 1843, he met in

Liverpool a fellow Jew, a Rabbi from Thessalonica. Some months earlier the Rabbi's synagogue in northern Greece had been destroyed by fire, and he was on a tour of Western Europe to raise funds for the re-building. Moses was naturally delighted to help, and he put him in touch with a number of Jews in the town who were in a position to give assistance. Moses painted a vivid picture of the times he took his Rabbi friend on their visits: 'I well remember the crowds of idle men and children which his fine-flowing Eastern robes attracted towards us, when I used to accompany him in his rounds. We were followed by vast numbers from street to street.' At first Moses, never shy, felt very self-conscious of all the attention that this aroused. 'I have a particular dislike to be run after,' he says. The Greek Rabbi assured him that once he became used to it he would take it as a matter of course. 'But,' he said, 'it did by no means change my dislike to being pointed, stared and gazed at.' However, he goes on, 'would you believe it, I got quite used to it and when the work was finished and the Eastern individual left Liverpool I almost regretted my sudden reverse of notoriety.' The two men of course discussed Christianity and the Rabbi 'most strenuously opposed me all the time he was in Liverpool.' But to Moses' astonishment, just as he was leaving, his friend avowed his belief in Jesus of Nazareth as the true Messiah, and moreover, he 'vowed to promulgate those doctrines to his brethren at his native place.' Moses gave him three copies of the Hebrew New Testament and also several letters of introduction to friends in Dublin, the next port of call for the faltering Greek fund-raiser. With that they said their goodbyes, but by a strange twist of fate they were one day to meet again in a distant land, and in circumstances which even in the most fanciful work of fiction, would defy credibility.

During his time in Juvenal Street some sparks flew as a result of his 'Fundamentals' book. He was always ready to

stand corrected on points of fact, but would fight tena-
ciously whenever attacked on matters of belief and
principle. One who dared to take issue with him was the
anonymous Charlotte Elizabeth, who, writing in the
Christian Lady's Magazine (1843), challenged the opinions he
had expressed, addressing her letters to the Bishop of
Jerusalem, Michael Alexander, who had been consecrated
as the first Bishop of that see just two years before in 1841.
Bringing the Bishop into the affair caused Moses some
dismay. She had strongly argued against Moses' assertions
that converted Jews should reject such national statutes as
matters relating to Circumcision and the Passover. Moses
would have none of it, addressing her dismissively as 'dear
lady', and pointing out that, by his arguments, it was clear
that modern Judaism did not reflect the religion of Moses
and the prophets, and these ancient usages should be
rejected by the convert.

Having as he thought gained the upper hand in this
literary skirmish, he continued teaching right up to June,
1844, when, on the 30th of that month, he was ordained in
St Peter's Liverpool, by the Bishop of Chester. It was a
dream come true, and to his delight, he was immediately
appointed to be curate at St Augustine's, Everton, a city
church sadly to be destroyed by enemy action nearly a
hundred years later, on the night of 4th May, 1941. The
Liverpool Record Office shows, for instance, that he was
taking services there in September and early October 1844,
but his stay in Liverpool was now destined to be of short
duration. In just a week or two he and his family were to
leave Liverpool and make their way to Dublin for the next
stage in his career.

His friend the Bishop of Kildare, third son of the fifth
Earl of Balcarres, and thirtieth Lord Lindsay of Crawford,
had in his gift the living of Glasnevin. In the 19th century
this was a parish and village in the Barony of Coolock, in

44

the County of Dublin, and in the Province of Leinster. Not much more than a mile out of the city, it was small and rural, with a population of just a few hundred.[7] In the time that Moses was there, he had as parishioners many worthy families, and there were a number of handsome houses in the village to accommodate them. Amongst the several well known names to have occupied Glasnevin in the past were Swift, Sheridan, Parnell and Addison. The property formerly belonging to the poet Tickell was destined one day to become the site of the now famous Botanical Gardens of the Royal Dublin Society. Moses was always interested in the process of printing, and it was appropriate that in Delville, another of the parish's grand houses and formerly the seat of the Revd Dr Delany, Dean of Down, were found the remains of a clandestine printing press used by Swift to produce his satires on the Irish Parliament. Not the least imposing of these properties which littered the parish was Glasnevin House, seat of his friend the Bishop of Kildare. Also within the parish boundaries was 'Claremont', an extensive institution founded in 1816 to house and educate deaf and dumb children between the inclusive ages of eight and twelve. Through the parish ran the river Tolka, and many of these fine houses, built on the northern bank of the river, enjoyed magnificent views of the countryside around. Early this century the church was described as a small structure, rebuilt in 1707 except for the tower, which is 'overspread with ivy'.

Bishop Lindsay had been impressed by young Margoliouth's intellect and personality and so, aware of his abilities and qualifications, he wrote to him, offering him the living of Glasnevin and, at the same time, said he

---

[7] The small church, the site of Christian worship for fifteen hundred years, is dedicated to St Mobhi, d. AD543, who founded a Christian community there and became Abbot and Bishop. The church building was enlarged in 1896 and 1908. The tower is fourteenth century.

Tower of Glasnevin Church, fourteenth century.

wished to appoint him his Examining Chaplain. Just four months after his ordination, this was advancement indeed, and Moses accepted at once. A further responsibility arrived at this time: just before leaving Liverpool, Chaja gave birth to a son, Charles Lindsay. So, his wife and two children with him, the Reverend Moses Margoliouth was licensed as Rector of Glasnevin on 23rd October 1844, and for nearly three years he and his family were to enjoy the luxury of a comfortable rectory, and he would preside over a small, easily run parish where he could pursue his writing and academic interests with comparative freedom and with the approval and protection of his patrician patron.

From this distance in time, it is hard to penetrate the mists that swirl around his private life. Equally, it is difficult to assess his financial affairs. His parents were still living, and maybe an allowance from his father was winging its way west. It is certainly likely that, with his stipend as rector of Glasnevin combined with whatever his post with the Bishop brought him, his professional income was higher than at any other stage in his life.

During his time there, he came back to Liverpool on several occasions, giving (in 1845) a series of lectures on the 'History of the Jews in Great Britain'. Interestingly, he apologised for 'my lisping broken accents' which are due to the fact that 'it is comparatively but a short time since I began to pay attention to your language and literature.' To illustrate the great pride he felt in his race and forbears he said in this same lecture, 'The history of the Jews... stands indeed associated with all that is sublime in the history of mankind.' He pointed out that lack of recorded history in mediaeval times was due to 'severe ill-usages which have been their painful lot to encounter.' He could hardly have imagined the ill-usages which were to be endured a century later.

As a Christian Jew he inevitably had battles with his own

people. One such skirmish was with a Dr Benisch, whom he detested. Moses had been for a time the honorary secretary of what was called the Philo-Hebraic Society. As a logo on top of its prospectus was a picture of Maimonides, the famous Rabbi of the twelfth and thirteenth centuries. Moses considered he had proof of its provenance and that it was an authentic likeness. He wrote: 'I take here the opportunity of doing myself a little act of justice which was unjustly denied me by those from whom I had reason to expect it. When I printed the prospectus, a copy seems to have found its way into the hands of Dr Benisch, the editor of the *Voice of Jacob* – a journal now defunct', he is pleased to say – 'a journal in which I was several times ABUSED IN A VERY SUMMARY MANNER'. Dr Benisch wanted to have details of its authenticity which Moses readily gave him. Moses goes on, 'Dr Benisch in no way acknowledged the information and help I gave him.' He adds, 'No, no – I am a Christian Jew and an apostate.' This was no petty quarrel; it was a long-term feud and Moses was determined to put before the public his side of the story.

Moses did rather enjoy this literary in-fighting. It was also at this time that he crossed swords with Moses Samuel, a distinguished nineteenth century Hebraist,[8] also Polish-born, and a resident of Liverpool for much of his life. Samuel is best remembered for his masterly translation of the works of Moses Mendelssohn the renowned eighteenth century Jewish writer and philosopher – a leading figure in the Enlightenment, and much admired by Moses Margoliouth.[9] Moses Samuel considered that some

---

[8] His family founded the famous high street jewellers, H. Samuel, although throughout his life Moses Samuel himself struggled unsuccessfully with his watchmakers shop in Paradise Street, Liverpool.

[9] Moses Samuel, in speaking of Mendelssohn, described 'the pleasing ductility of his most exquisite cogitations,' and also alluded to him as 'the grand luminary of science and knowledge'.

medieval English Jews – notably those known as 'the Wise Men of Norwich' had contributed a substantial degree of philosophical scholarship to Talmudic thought. Moses Margoliouth considered this to be historical nonsense and arranged for his opinions to be printed in the Jewish Chronicle, challenging Samuel to produce concrete argument for his assertion, which he failed to do. In addition to their obvious religious divergence, this affair caused a permanent rift between the two men. (To this day the merits of the Norwich theory are still subject to controversy.)

In July 1846 he was especially pleased and honoured to be granted the privilege of reading in the TCD library. This was conferred on him at the recommendation of Dr Singer and Dr Todd, two of the College senior teaching staff. He took every opportunity to take advantage of this helpful gesture. Then, the following month brought sadness – on 8th August the Bishop of Kildare died.[10] The loss of this man, so like a character out of Trollope, was a blow to Moses but in no way did it mark the end of his connections with the Lindsay family. He remained on close terms with his son and heir, Capt. George Hayward Lindsay, and his wife Lady Mary, who was sister to the Earl of Arran. George Lindsay inherited Glasnevin House, and he and his wife continued to show kindness and hospitality towards their rector and friend.

Knowing the Lindsays had given him entry into Dublin society, and at their home he associated with an assortment of local gentry, fellow intellectuals and visiting politicians from across the water.[11] One day in 1846 he met there Sir Thomas Francis Fremantle (later Lord Cottesloe), Secretary for Ireland. He intriguingly reappears briefly later in this

---

[10] He was buried in the cathedral of Christchurch, Dublin.

[11] Notably amongst the latter was the Earl of Clarendon – see p.63.

story.

At this time, either in Liverpool or, more probably, in Dublin, he became a Freemason. For a comparatively brief period he was extremely keen on 'the craft' which contained elements greatly appealing to his interests in antiquity and archaeology. He was by nature a literalist, and by modern standards perhaps read too much into the signs and symbols which he was convinced stretched back to the days of King Solomon and the building of the Temple. In a year or two he would become a member of three lodges in Lancashire and Cheshire, but his later peripatetic lifestyle made it impossible for him to maintain his enthusiasm, and his interest waned.

For a short period ambition was assuaged, and the life of their rector must have appeared to the parishioners of Glasnevin to be a picture of domestic bliss, so deserved, they thought, after long years of study and effort: and again Chaja was pregnant which served to emphasise the joy and contentment which surely lay between the walls of Glasnevin Rectory. But behind the facade all was not as it appeared. Domestic tensions had returned, and tragedy was about to enter the lives of the Margoliouths. A baby boy was born and christened Lancelot Lindsay, but the infant barely survived its baptism, and the whole episode brought to the parents feelings of anguish and loss. (Perhaps at this time Miriam was also baptised, now adding in the ceremony the names of the Bishop's widow: Miriam became Miriam Esther Naomi Catherine Lindsay Margoliouth).

As a diversion, in January 1847, Moses tried his hand at a publishing venture. The *Star of Jacob* was a monthly magazine which ran for six months, and perhaps was an attempt to be one up on Dr Benisch, but by the time the last issue had been printed in June, he was approaching a further milestone in his life. After much consideration – part escape, and undoubtedly with some encouragement from his father – he was about to fulfil another ambition: he would visit the Holy Land – and with this project in view he resigned the living of Glasnevin.

Perhaps his small parish was insufficiently demanding. It was certainly a disappointment to him when the Archbishop of Dublin made himself Bishop of Kildare following Bishop Lindsay's death, combining the two posts – an arrangement which continued until the Archbishop's death in 1863. It seems fairly certain too that his marriage was again failing – in truth it had probably never succeeded. The fact is that he had decided to go abroad, and he bade farewell to the Lindsays, the Crawford family of Carlingford House, the elderly Lady Powerscourt, the Wilsons of Churchill, his Lordship's butler Miller, who had so often served him wine off the Lindsay silver, and all the other Glasnevin parishioners whose souls had been under his care for this brief interlude.

Perhaps Chaja Margoliouth was the cause of it all. Was she a thoroughly bad lot, like the wife of the Prophet Hosea? Did she taunt him with her conquests and scream at him in the small hours when he preached to her of the need to repent? There is some evidence for the prosecution – it is not compelling, but it does exist. Or was she a pale, wronged and abandoned woman, tear-stained and broken hearted? For her part, she rests her case. Not a syllable is heard on behalf of the defence, and until the family received news of her illness and death in France, she disappears from view. The children however figure dramatically later in the story after remaining for years like ghosts in a corridor. But their mother, with hardly a backward glance, disappears into the sunset.

Chapter III
The Pilgrimage: Part One

The details of his 'Pilgrimage' have been gleaned from a series of letters which he wrote to relatives and friends from various points on his journey. There is no interconnecting narrative, so one must make sense of a somewhat disjointed sequence to form the whole. Two further matters should be clarified – there is no doubt that he had left his wife, but this fact was concealed, not only from the outside world, but also from those nearest to the couple. It would have been impossible, in the climate of the time, for a clergyman to pursue a career in the church (which Moses did), against a background of domestic irregularity. The fact is that he left Dublin to explore North Africa and Palestine and, naturally, he couldn't take his family too. In later years his wife would be away attending to the education of the children, or looking after relatives, or whatever; there would be no hint of scandal.

Referring to the cost of the trip, there is no sign of indebtedness in any of the letters he wrote, using his 'Wedgewood'.[1] He had many friends of substance – the Lindsay family for instance, and Sir Thomas Baring[2], the

---

[1] A patented device for making copies; obviously later superseded by carbon paper.

[2] The family were eminent London merchants and bankers. Sir Thomas was the second baronet. His eldest son Francis became the first Baron Northbrook. How Moses knew Sir Thomas is not clear. However, Sir Thomas's fourth son, Charles, was ordained and became Bishop of

banker, but in correspondence with these people there is no hint of benevolence on their part. He was a year away and the project must have been costly. The conclusion has to be drawn that his father supplied the means. He (Gershon) was, after all, getting something in return – letters, information, especially from Metz and, later on, from Jerusalem, and probably a promise that his son would one day produce an account of his trip. This he did, in 1850, in the form of the many copy letters he possessed, with added details from what he called his evening notes, the whereabouts of which, if they still exist, are unknown.

The first part of his plan was to reach Tunis,[3] where he had arranged to stay with a converted Jew, one Nathan Davis, and his wife Catherine. They were newly-weds, and with all the enthusiasm of their youth they were trying to establish a Christian mission there. Catherine Davis, née Brown, was the step-daughter of his friend Henry Joseph, and this meeting had been arranged with the Josephs during detailed discussions back in Cheshire, in Rose Bank Cottage. The whole enterprise was to be the trip of a lifetime. It was, in a way, like leaving Suwalki, in that he was again a free man. He set out in early July 1847, crossing to Liverpool and, as always, called in to see the Josephs at Chester. From there he went on to London, where he spent a day or two sightseeing, including an inspection of Westminster Abbey, but, anxious to press on, he crossed the channel and was soon in Paris which, for several weeks, was to be his base, staying at Meurice's hotel.

He rather disapproved of the French capital, where Sundays were treated as days of jollity and games, and he

---

Bristol and Gloucester, 1856-61, and of Durham, 1861-79. It could be that Moses knew Charles from his time at TCD, and therefore through him had contact with his father.

[3] There is evidence that he intended to visit Spain, but finances did not permit.

complained that the Parisian women paraded the streets in their finery in order to attract attention. The fair sex understandably was not high in his estimation at this time. He said, 'As long as my eyes rest exclusively upon the majestic and august buildings and monuments... the libraries [he visited thirty of them] colleges and museums, I feel charmed. The people and the nation as a whole give rise to feelings of an antagonistic nature'. Some of his antagonism was aimed at the Roman Church, 'which is very bad indeed'.

Most days he spent at least some time in the various libraries, being anxious to gain as much knowledge as possible to prepare himself for the trip. However, he considered, somewhat uncharitably, that the British Museum and the Bodleian were far superior. He was particularly fascinated by the famous obelisk which stood, and still stands, in the Place de la Concorde. It had come from Luxor, he told his friends, and he went to see it most days to examine its carved hieroglyphics. This sort of thing was very much what his journey was about, and in a letter to the Archbishop of Dublin he gives the principle reason for his trip: 'Besides investigating the present state of Christians, Jews, Turks, Infidels and Heretics, I am also anxious to make an attempt at deciphering the famous inscriptions in the deserts of Arabia, which are found on the rocks surrounding the valley now known by the name of Wady (Wadi) Mokatteb[4]. Those inscriptions have hitherto defied the ingenuity and learning of all archaeological travellers'.

He will, he says, always remember his dear Glasnevin friends. In writing to Lady Mary Lindsay he tells her that he

---

[4] This is probably Wadi Mukattem, which is in Jordan, not far from the Dead Sea, about midway between Amman and Petra. It appears this projected visit did not take place.

had recently met Lord Lindsay,[5] a kinsman of the old Bishop, who had been staying at St Germains. Lord Lindsay's knowledge of the Middle East and its history was considerable, and he and Moses had long discussions on the antiquities of Syria and Palestine. For Moses it was a useful and instructive meeting. He goes on to tell Lady Mary that whilst they were in an animated and absorbing conversation, a third person tried to join in. Lord Lindsay shouted, 'We are deep in Syria and must not be interrupted!' Moses was in his element.

He could always produce a sermon at the drop of a hat and on one of the Sundays in August he preached at the request of the Revd R. Lovell, the pastor in the Episcopal Chapel. In the congregation were the Duke and Duchess of Manchester[6] with their son and daughter. They were

---

[5] Lord Lindsay (1787-1851) was Sir Henry Lindsay-Bethune, Bart. He entered the East India Company at an early age and was sent from Madras to Persia to assist Abbas Mirza, the Crown Prince, in organising his artillery. He became celebrated throughout the Empire for ability and gallantry, and he was also an acknowledged expert on historical and archaeological matters relating to the near and middle east. He subsequently served as accredited agent to the Persian Court. He inherited the Lindsay title in 1839.

[6] 6th Duke of Manchester, George Montagu, b. 9th July, 1799. The Duchess was his first wife – Millicent (d. 21st Nov. 1848), only daughter and heiress of Brig. Gen. Robert Bernard Sparrow, of Brampton Park, Huntingdon. Their silent son, Lord Mandeville, was William Drogo Montagu, (1823-1890). He succeeded his father as 7th Duke in 1855. Lord Mandeville married in 1852 the Countess Louise Fredericke Auguste, daughter of the Comte d'Alten of Hanover. (She later, in 1892, married the 8th Duke of Devonshire. The 'double duchess' was, in her younger days considered a great beauty – 'no one knows how gloriously beautiful a woman can be who did not see the Duchess of Manchester when she was thirty'. She brought new life and much social whirl to Chatsworth which had been without a duchess for eighty years. She died in 1911.) The daughter of the Manchesters to whom MM alludes was Olivia, b. c. 1830. In 1850 she married the 6th Earl of Tankerville. She lived on until 1922.

staying at the Hotel Bristol, and they asked Moses to call round as they would like to meet him and in particular to discuss the Hebrew language and its literature in which the Duchess was especially interested. Moses told her that he hoped to visit Spain, and the Duchess gave him a letter of introduction to Mr Brackenbury, the British Consul in Cadiz. Although he didn't reach Spain, this indicates the original extent of his ambitions. Moses accepted their invitation and to his amusement the son and heir (Lord Mandeville) was demonstrably bored with the whole thing. 'He was clearly the silent type,' says Moses. 'He gave his organs of speech a thorough good rest.' His hostess, on being told of his intended route from France, gave him a letter of introduction to the Bishop of Gibraltar, who then resided in Malta, which was to prove useful to him.

In September, almost exactly ten years late, he left Paris to pay a short visit to Metz on his father's behalf. He wrote to Suwalki to say that in 1829 a Rabbinical College was established there and 'it recommends itself to your benevolence'. In view of this suggestion he goes on to give details of its condition, output and financial affairs. At the same time he tells his family that they in turn must reply with an up-to-date assessment of 'the future prospects of our nation scattered through Russia and Poland.'

Before the month was out, he was back in Paris having felt that he had discharged his duties, at least for the time being, towards his family. Now the time had come to travel south and he set out for Marseilles, travelling as far as Orleans by train.[7] He had with him a number of letters of introduction, including one from the Revd Lovell of Paris to M. Rosselloty, Protestant minister in Orleans, but

---

[7] It was only south to Orleans (and then west to Tours and Angers) that the railway system had been completed at this time, although a more extensive network of lines was then under construction throughout France.

although it afforded him some help, M. Rosselloty himself was away. As usual, he explored the churches and museums, in one museum finding a very fine antique chest carved with a scene depicting David and Solomon. The cathedral he found magnificent, and spent several hours there before setting out by train for Bourges. He met in the carriage three German students who turned out to be Jews. They were loathe to admit their race, they said, owing to prejudice. By pure chance they shared the same hotel in Bourges and the four of them stayed one night there. In the hotel was a Roman Catholic bishop who, the following morning, proudly showed them round Bourges cathedral, the west facade of which Moses found particularly fine, with figures portraying the Last Judgement.

From Bourges he travelled to Roanne where again he stayed one night at an inn, and then left by diligence for Lyon. There he remained for several days and spent his time wandering round the town and, of course, examining closely the various churches, the cathedral and the amphitheatre. One day he climbed the high tower adjacent to the church of Notre Dame de Fourvières, from the top of which he had the most clear and extensive views of the surrounding countryside; he claimed he could see Mont Blanc away to the east.

From Lyon he took a steamer on the Rhone to Avignon and, to his delight, he met up again with his three Jewish student friends. The four of them were able to renew their conversations and, at the same time, view the wonderful scenery on either side of the river. Soon they were in Avignon, and from there they took a coach to Marseilles.

It was still September and now in Marseilles he said goodbye to the three Germans and booked in at the Hotel des Empereurs. He was now in the port which he thought compared unfavourably with Liverpool and once again he set out on his tour of the place. He was told that recently (in June 1845), two vast stones had been unearthed during the demolition of an old house. They were extensively carved with hieroglyphics and had been placed on view in the Marseilles museum. Moses went hot-foot to look at them and with great excitement wrote to Dr James McCullagh at TCD (obviously a fellow-devotee of such things), telling him that the writing was Phoenician, detailing a 'code of laws respecting the rites of sacrifices, and the rights of the priests' borrowed, he explained, from the Book of Leviticus. Next he visited the Church of St Victor ('I do not own him as my favourite saint') and described the church itself as inferior to most of the fine ecclesiastical buildings he had so far been visiting in France. He also looked round the Chapel of Notre Dame de la Garde. He wrote to his friend William Titherington of Chester, a cotton broker in Liverpool:[8] 'The Chapel possesses some interest by reason of the respect which it inspires in the estimation of sailors and their wives, fisher-men and their wives – it is very rich in the enjoyment of extraordinary relics and trophies, which would make you smile and sigh at the same time'. Amongst the curiosities in the Chapel, he catalogues: 'an image of the Virgin Mary carved in olive wood, and of great antiquity; the walls of the chapel, as well as the roof, are concealed by the vast number of *ex votos,* principally paintings, representing moving accidents by flood and field, justly characterised as the veriest daubs. Besides a vast number of shipwrecks, storms, steam-boat explosions, escapes from British frigates, there is a large collection of surgical operations, sick beds, road-side accidents. Many ostrich eggs and models of ships are suspended from the roof, and one corner is filled with cast-off crutches, etc.' He goes on to tell his Liverpool friend that from a distance the harbour of Marseilles is beautiful

---

[8] Another possible candidate to have been Moses' benefactor in 1840.

but, close to, it is the 'sewer of the city'. He added, 'Twenty thousand vessels come and go each year.'

Still in Marseilles he attended the Protestant chapel and, in his professional opinion, listened to an 'able sermon'. Whereas Moses had frowned on the women parading the streets of Paris he equally disapproved of excessive piety. In his hotel, he heard an elderly Quaker admonish a young man for over-indulgence – for listening to too much music, drinking too much wine, and wearing too much 'Rowland's Macassar'. He commented: 'Why shouldn't a young man enjoy music, wine and hair-cream!'

It was the month of the Marseilles fiesta, and he went to see a caricature in wax of the British Privy Council! He continued to express disapproval of the French, even attacking French Jews who had market stalls selling – 'what do you think? Why! Crosses, crucifixes and all sorts of Roman Catholic household Gods.'

Before September was out, he set sail early one beautiful morning on the French steamer *Le Bosphore*. He was on his way to Italy.

★

In those days the Italian town of Livorno (Leghorn) was a regular port of call for ships on the route south from Marseilles – it was a twenty-six hour journey between the two. As always, Moses gave details to his friends back home of any interesting people he met on his travels, and there were oddities aplenty. For nearly twelve months his many exotic encounters were to be a world away from the staid aristocratic society he had known in Dublin. On *Le Bosphore* he first came across an Armenian who at one time had acted as interpreter for the Bishop of Jerusalem;[9] now

---

[9] Bishop Michael Alexander, the first Bishop appointed in 1841.

he was working in the service of the Pasha of Alexandria and had been to London taking in his charge twelve young men whom the Pasha had sent to attend college there and now he was returning home.[10] Also on board was the Pasha's favourite wife with her entourage, all under the care and jurisdiction of a Mullah. The latter discussed the New Testament with Moses, and seeing that he had a version in Arabic, asked if he could have it. Moses reluctantly gave it to him – it was his only copy. Another interesting character he met on the ship was a Signor Molini, head librarian in Florence, with whom Moses had a series of enlightening talks – one in particular about the printing processes and the machinery used in that part of the world – a subject which always held a special fascination for him.

Also on board *Le Bosphore*, adding to the kaleidoscopic cast-list about him, were about one hundred and fifty Bedouin Arabs on their way to Mecca. They proved troublesome, and the Captain punished some of them by tying them to the masts – Moses heartily approved of this. Then one of the Pasha's servants, a Negro, became insolent and 'refractory' – he was also tied up and flogged, again to Moses' satisfaction – it was a fair and just punishment and a lesson to the rest.

Eventually, after all this excitement, they finally docked at Leghorn. Almost immediately he was witness to an incident in the port which he found disturbing: a Jesuit was being persecuted by a mob, and he escaped from the clutches of the crowd just in time by taking refuge in the house of a priest. 'As Christian society is so extremely riotous,' he said, 'I betook myself to the Jewish quarter.' In a letter which he wrote to the Bishop of Down and Connor at this time he gave extensive details of the history of the

---

[10] Eight of the students were studying political economy, and four, mechanical engineering – progressive choices.

Jews in that part of Italy. He said that there were always signs of anti-Semitic feeling. Lately Rabbis were forced to dress up as Catholic priests to avoid persecution, so that when he sees someone 'in that fantastic garb' he doesn't know whether he is a priest or a Rabbi. Recently a Jewish school had been established in Leghorn, but rich Jews still sent their children to the Christian schools. This, he felt was very sad. The synagogue, he said, was magnificent – a fine and richly adorned building, possessing no less than sixty splendid Torahs (parchment scrolls of the Pentateuch), and 'hundreds of chandeliers' presumably from Venice.

From Leghorn he had time briefly to visit Pisa and Florence, for which towns it serves as the port. He was sorry to discover that the Hebrew printing presses of both towns had been lost. He considered as one would expect that the architecture was wonderful and, like every tourist, he climbed up the 'famous belfry'. He amusingly reported that 'the sensation I experienced was of so disagreeable a nature that I have not as yet got over it!'

His time was limited amidst these delights, and he was soon on board another French steamer on the next leg of his journey, to Malta; a trip of some three and a half days. He was now to experience his first serious danger – a violent Mediterranean storm. He gave a dramatic account in a letter which he sent to the Archbishop of Canterbury, no less. 'All was calm,' he says, when suddenly 'the billows in their strength dashed furiously over our bark, and the shrieks of an affrighted crew rivalled the noise of the mighty waters... but thanks be to the Captain of our Salvation, who brought us out this morning from our distress. He made the sea calm, so that the waves thereof are still; and all on board seem grateful to their mighty Deliverer. This circumstance furnished a deeply interesting subject for conversation amongst the passengers.' The

reason for writing to the Archbishop was to reply to a query
– could he, Moses, confirm that Malta was the Melita
where St Paul was shipwrecked (Acts 28:1). Lord Lindsay,
an acknowledged expert on such matters, considered that it
was not – Melita was the island of Meleda in the Adriatic; a
theory, at the time, preferred by many. For this reason
Moses told His Grace that he had been in the same scepti-
cal frame of mind, but he had come to the conclusion that
it *was* Malta – basing his argument on wind direction, and
the fact that Malta was on the most likely and straightfor-
ward course to Rome.

Arriving at last on this lovely and strategically placed
Mediterranean island, his first letter was to 'My Dearest
Miriam.' He writes: 'You will no doubt be looking out for a
letter from your papa from this pretty little island and I
should be very sorry indeed to disappoint you. But the
difficulty I have to contend with is the choosing of a
suitable subject for an epistle to a young lady at school.' He
tells her that he goes each day for a sail which costs 4d. In
these trips round the bay he could enjoy wonderful views
of the town and harbour of Valetta. He was staying at
Baker's Princess Royal hotel which was situated in the main
square. Soon, by means of the letter he possessed from the
Duchess of Manchester he was able to meet the Bishop of
Gibraltar, the Rt Revd Dr Tomlinson whose diocese, he
tells Miriam, includes Rome and extends east/west from
Constantinople (Istanbul) to Aporto in Portugal. The
beautiful and elegant church in Valetta was built largely
thanks to the 'benevolent and pious Queen Adelaide', (wife
of William IV). He interestingly goes on to tell her that the
church organ 'which once sounded the praises of Jehovah
in the Cathedral of Chester, is now doing the same here,
and perhaps louder than ever. It appears that its Chester
friends thought it in a rapid decline, and therefore sent it
abroad. I know not to what the change may be ascribed,

62

whether to the long sea voyage, or the mildness of the climate, but I know it has renewed its youth and vigour, like the fabled Phoenix, and therefore it is as melodious as ever.'[11]

He preached a sermon in Queen Adelaide's church, and also attended worship in the Palace Chapel which was used by the forces, but also was well attended by civilians. The Chaplain there was the Revd W. Hare. 'I know his brother in Dublin very well, and we therefore have a little interesting chat now and then.' Of course, he also visited the synagogue. 'It is on the third storey in the last house on the south side of Strada Reale.'

At the point of leaving Malta, he was annoyed to be delayed for two weeks by a quarantine restriction, but at least it gave him more time for sightseeing. Then, at last, he set sail once more, this time on board the *Scotia* bound for Tunis, passing the island of Pantelloria, and arriving in 'the bay known as the Goletta' on October 18th. He recorded that on the day of his arrival the English steam-frigate the *Antelope* docked with a 'sumptuous present' – a horse-drawn carriage – from 'our Beloved Queen' to the 'much disliked' Bey of Tunis. The *Antelope* was immediately returning to Malta so he could send his letters back there to be posted for him by an Irish barrister, appropriately named Mr Ireland, whom he had met on the quayside; this would save both time and expense.

Tunis was a vital stop on his travels as he was keen to inspect the many ancient sites which were situated in the locality, in particular the ruins of the ancient city of

---

[11] This extract is an indication of his sense of humour, and the tone seems exactly appropriate for a letter sent to a young lady of twelve; it ties in with other evidence of the date of Miriam's birth. It also suggests that *perhaps* the Margoliouth children were living in Cheshire. The author has been unable to trace any letter to, or mention of, Chaja Margoliouth during his time away.

Carthage. As planned through the Josephs, he there met up with Nathan and Catherine Davis (see appendices). The Revd Nathan Davis was in Tunis working as a missionary under the auspices of the Church of Scotland. Not only was Catherine Davis (née Brown) the step-daughter of his friend Henry Joseph, she was also the sister of John Brown (later the Revd John M. Brown), a close friend of Moses from his time in Dublin, and to whom he wrote from Tunis giving details of his adventures in North Africa; in 1847–8 John Brown was still a student at TCD prior to ordination. Moses stayed with Nathan and Catherine during his time in Tunis, and he helped out with the pastoral work there, by taking services and generally working in the 'parish'. They were making do with a temporary building – a church and school were still on the drawing board.[12] Moses greatly admired the work of his host and hostess, who were struggling under adverse circumstances.

Before he left Dublin he had, through the Earl of Clarendon, received several letters of introduction from Lord Palmerston,[13] and he felt the time had come to thank his Lordship. In a letter to him, he said, 'I purpose staying here some time, as I am anxious to make myself thoroughly well acquainted with the present state of this wretched regency, as regards its civil, political, literary and religious condition'. He goes on to tell Lord Palmerston that Tunis and its area is a 'long de-graded region'. He also adds 'I have obtained a good deal of information about the real

---

[12] It was never built. Some years later he wrote: 'In consequence of unbecoming jealousy and want of protection on the part of the authorities, the mission of the chapel and schools were abandoned and the Protestants and Jews of Tunis are once more destitute as ever of any religious instruction.

[13] Lord Palmerston, 3rd Earl, had been appointed Foreign Secretary the previous year, 1846, in Lord Russell's administration.

state of the interior of Africa and... I purpose to communicate to your Lordship the information I may collect during that part of my pilgrimage.'[14]

He also wrote to his recently acquired friend the Bishop of Gibraltar, warmly endorsing the work of Nathan Davis – this was to counteract the assessment of Sir Thomas Reade, British Consul in Tunis, who had not spoken well of him. 'I am also happy to be able to inform you that Mr Davis consents to my having full service of the Church of England in his temporary chapel once a fortnight.' And he adds, 'Mr Davis has been the means of rescuing several Romanists from the thraldom of the papacy.' He also told the Bishop: 'Experience in missionary work amongst the Jews convinces me that no Church who does not possess so beautiful and scriptural a Liturgy as ours should attempt to make converts amongst the Jews.' This remark is both self-revelatory and highly significant. It shows his love and respect for the Church of England Orders of Service, now so often discarded.

During his short stay in London, Moses had met and received kindness from one W.C. Townsend, a QC who had asked him to let him have some information about the judicial system in Tunis. Moses obliged: 'The Bey acted as judge, and the cases were pleaded before him. His Highness' decision is fulfilled there and then without... appeal'. On the other hand, 'Capital executions do but seldom occur.'

From the Davis' house where he was staying, he had, he told Lord Lindsay, a vivid picture across the adjoining plain of the remains of the ancient city of Carthage. 'All is in ruin, an area once covered with magnificent palaces, majestic edifices and lofty towers surrounded by mighty

---

[14] For reasons which will become apparent, he abandoned further exploration into the interior of North Africa.

and almost invincible triple walls, yet I could stand motionless for hours and muse over the dreary and silent scene. There is a sort of bewitching charm in the landscape, which rivets my eyes immovably on the panorama, though the effect it produces upon me is a very melancholy one'. He then tells his Lordship of the recent discovery of a fine white marble female head. 'It is as big as myself altogether.' He goes on to explain that the British Vice-Consul, a Mr Ferriere (serving under Sir Thos. Reade) had made a sketch of himself standing beside the head, 'a copy of which I enclose herewith.'[15] He tells his Lordship that he thinks it is the head of the empress Theodora, wife of Justinian. He thought this theory plausible but modestly hastened to assure his Lordship 'However I never feel annoyed in the least when people choose to differ from me.' He also explained that the head 'was found on 10th August, 1847,' perfect timing for him, and at the request of the French Ambassador, the Bey had decided to give it to the French nation and it was to be housed in the 'Museum of Paris.'[16]

---

[15] See illustration, p.66. No doubt due to his seniority in years, Moses always referred to him as 'Mr Ferriere'. According to the Foreign Office lists, he was Lewis Ferriere, and was a clerk in the War Office from September, 1810 to May, 1832, when he retired on a pension. His experience was clearly appreciated, and he was brought out of retirement to be appointed Vice Consul in Tunis in August, 1841 until 1849. He acted later as the British Agent and Consul General in Tunis for three short periods: June, 1849 to March, 1850; March to June, 1855; and from July, 1855 to June, 1856. He finally retired on a superannuation allowance in December, 1856.

[16] It is in the Louvre, which corrects Moses' attribution: 'The colossal head you are talking about in your letter is a head of the Empress Lucilla, wife of Lucius Verus. It was found during excavations made to build a chapel amid the ruins of Carthage. In fact it was built on the ruins of a basilica to Lucius Verus and his wife. Only the head remains. The head belongs to an 'acrolithe', so called because only the head, the hands and the feet are made of marble – the rest was made of wood. The approximate date, because of the style of the headdress, is AD160.

Reverend Moses Margoliouth with carved head of the Empress Lucilla
by Lewis Ferriere, British Vice-Consul at Tunis. Drawn in 1847.

The 18th December was one of the main Tunisian festivals and he was invited to attend along with the American Consul,[17] a levée given at the Bey's palace. He considered it a decadent affair. He commented again to Lord Lindsay, 'The whole of this regency is on the brink of ruin and all through the mal-government of the reigning Bey.' Thinking of his plans away in the future he said in a letter at this time to the Duchess of Manchester, 'I may perhaps leave for Alexandria in September next, as earlier would be too hot.'[18]

So far his letters sent back home entertained many friends and often brought smiles to their faces as they sat by their winter firesides. His words brought sunshine, and at the same time a touch of magic to those he had left behind in Dublin, Chester, Liverpool and Poland. But soon his news was to take a different tone – he would be giving an account of a disaster which was about to strike with horror the British public, and in which Moses himself became involved, practically and emotionally, and which was to affect the future course of his pilgrimage.

---

[17] Samuel D. Heap.

[18] Shortage of both time and money prevented him from carrying out this part of his plan.

Chapter IV
Disaster at Sea

While Moses and his friends were safely in Tunis, Captain Charles George Edward Napier was in command of Her Majesty's Steamship *Avenger* as it set sail from Gibraltar on 17th December, 1847. It was a Paddle Frigate, tonnage 1,444bm[1] and measured 210 x 39 feet. It had been built in Devonport Dockyard, Plymouth just over two years before, and was launched on 5th August, 1845. At the start of this stage of its voyage, on its way to Malta, the weather was fine and calm, but by the 20th, a Monday, as evening drew on, conditions deteriorated. To quote the statement of one of its officers, Lieut. Francis Rooke:

> On the Monday evening last, Dec. 20th, when the wind was very high and the sea very rough, the *Avenger* in which I served as Lieutenant, and which was on her way to Malta, was contending for mastery over the raging billows and roaring waves in the then angry Mediterranean. As for myself, having been a sailor from my youth, and possessing much confidence in the great powers of the *Avenger*, I went down into the cabin and amused myself by playing a rubber of whist with a friend. Whilst thus engaged, I heard a

---

[1] Bm = Builder's Measure; a capacity measurement arrived at by calculating the number of tuns (casks) of wine that a ship could carry. This system was discontinued in 1873.

violent shock, upon which I exclaimed, 'A fine piece of work! there is a cannon got loose.' I hastened on deck and, whilst running, I heard another shock, a more violent one than the former. As soon as I got on board, I heard the Captain (Napier) saying, 'Get you down the best way you can, and how you can!' I saw the steamer was going to pieces; I let down, therefore, one of the boats and entered with seven fellow servants of that steamer, one of whom was the physician. As soon as we were in the boat, a boisterous billow flung us at a considerable distance from the unfortunate *Avenger*. I heard, however, loud shrieks and screams from her crew, and in a few moments she went into perdition – she was dashed into pieces on a coral reef between the island of Galeta and Tabarca. This happened about ten o'clock of that painfully memorable evening. My seven companions and myself were tossed the whole night by the capricious storm and sea in a most merciless manner. We expected every moment to be added to the number of our comrades – two hundred and fifty – at the bottom of the sea. The fatal foreboding was at last realised – our little bark was shattered, and we were all plunged into the ocean, not being able even to seize hold of a plank. I know not what became of four of my fellow-sailors – I conclude that they were drowned; as for myself and these three individuals, consisting of a mate, midshipman, and an inferior sailor, it appears we were washed ashore between Biserta and Tabarca almost lifeless. An Arab found us in that state, and kindly conveyed us to his hospitable tent, and with fostering hand fanned in us the almost extinguished vital spark, to life again. For we remember nothing of our struggle from the time our little boat was upset till the time we found ourselves in the

Arab's tent. As soon as my friends and myself felt capable of moving again, we made ourselves understood by signs – for we knew not a word of the Arabic language – that we escaped from a frightful wreck, and begged him to bring us to a place where an English Consul resided. He conducted us to Biserta where Mr Manucci, the English Vice-Consul, furnished us with a boat, in which we made our way to the Goletta in order to inform the British Consul-General of Tunisia of the sad catastrophe that had befallen Her Britannic Majesty's steamer, and to procure some help for the purpose of visiting that destructive part where her ruin took place, peradventure we might find some mutilated bodies of our forlorn friends.

News had spread like wildfire through Tunis, and the extent of the disaster was soon confirmed – as many as two hundred and fifty of the crew had been lost. The four survivors were Lieut. Rooke, who gave the statement; John Larcom, Gunner; William Hill, midshipman and Captain's Steward; and James Morley, boy of the first class. They, with the help of an Arab who found them, managed to make their way to Tunis arriving on the Thursday night. Sir Thomas Reade immediately instructed Moses' artist friend Mr Ferriere 'to make every exertion to procure as much assistance as possible.' The Bey, obviously not all bad, supplied three ships and they, along with a French man-of-war steamer, the *Lavoisier*, set out to search the area. Nothing was found except a few barrels, a chair and a cabin door.

In order to play their part, and possibly at the request of Sir Thomas Reade, Moses and Nathan Davis at once left on horseback for Biserta, one of the nearest points on the mainland to the scene of the tragedy. The journey, some forty-five miles to the west, was a hazardous one due to brigands, and they went fully armed and accompanied by bodyguards. On reaching Biserta, Moses stayed there with rations and equipment while Mr Davis went a little further up the coast where two bodies were found on the beach. They were thought to have been lost from Lieut. Rooke's cutter and were buried at a place called Elakabaat, in the presence of forty-six Moslems, 'all of whom behaved with becoming decorum.'

One of the bodies was found wearing part of a shirt marked 'Ayling', and Lieut. Rooke later confirmed that this would be 'Mr Ayling, Master's Assistant, Drowned in Boat'. Moses wrote to Lady Mary Lindsay, somewhat optimistically: 'You may perhaps hear of some of his relations, or come in contact with some of them. It would be gratifying to afford them the information that their relative who was lost in the wreck of the *Avenger* was found by the Revd N. Davis of Tunis, and interred by the same Christian Minister in the regency of Tunis, at Sidi Mansoor at a place called Elakabaat beneath a wide spreading tree, resembling a weeping willow.' This message, if ever received by his family, must surely have given comfort. Mr Davis gave the following account of the same episode:

> After fourteen hours' ride on 1st January I reached the spot and found on the beach the body of a sailor. I placed a guard over the body; and as it was late I sought for shelter. The following day I found another body near the spot where the boat was upset in the surf. It was that of S. Ayling, as I afterwards discovered from a piece of his shirt, on which this name was in marking ink. These bodies were interred on 3rd January.

Then a day or two later another body was found, thought to

72

be that of the ship's doctor, and that too was properly buried with a short service of prayers and a hymn.

While the two clergymen were away on their painful tasks, Lieut. Rooke was giving more details of the catastrophe to his superiors. On Friday the 24th December he had written to Vice Admiral Sir William Parker[2] in Malta:

Tunis, Friday 8 a.m. (24th December, 1847)

Sir,
With sorrow I have to report to you the wreck of H.M. Steamer *Avenger* on a coral reef between the Island of Galita and the mainland, the Island bore about N.E. 10 or 12 miles at the time. The Ship was running with square yards and also under steam at the rate of 8 or 9 knots; she struck about 10 p.m. and in a few minutes was a wreck, her masts and funnel gone, she nearly on her beam ends with the sea beating over her. The Captain and Master were on the Paddle Box at the time; the Captain immediately giving the order (out boats), she having struck so heavily as to convince every body that the case was hopeless – the Master had taken bearings of a Cape on the Affrican (sic) shore. We arrived at Tunis last night at 12 p.m. when immediately sent four (sic) our Consul who came and began prepairng (sic) 2 Feluccas for me, there being no Steamer here. I called this morning on the Consul General Sir

---

[2] Sir William Parker 1st Bt. (1781-1866). A distinguished naval officer; he was one of the Lords of the Admiralty from July to December, 1834 and again from April, 1835 to May, 1841 when he resigned, and was nominated Commander-in Chief on the East India station. His subsequent gallant services in China obtained for him the Grand Cross of the Bath in 1842, and on 18th December, 1844 a patent of Baronetcy. Sir William was first ADC to the Queen and Senior Admiral of the Fleet.

Thomas Reade who is forwarding my views in every way. The Bey of Tunis has placed at my disposal one of his Brigs, and 2 Gun Boats, and I hope to be under weigh with them by 2 p.m. The French Steamer which is hourly expected will follow. I shall search Galita and go to the wreck; horsemen[3] will be sent along the African Coast and you may rest assured, Sir, everything possible shall be done although I do it more as a duty than thinking of saving the men, for both wind and sea were very high on Tuesday. If I can hear or see nothing of the Ship I shall then proceed to Malta to give further particulars.

I remain, Sir, &c.

(Signed) *Francis Rooke*,
3rd Lieutenant of HMS

Names of those saved in the Cutter:
Lieut. Rooke.
Mr Larkam (sic) Gunner.
Wm Hill (Steward).
Jas Morley (boy).
Drowned: (i.e. lost from the cutter).
Dr Steele
Mr Betts (2nd Master)
Mr Ayling (Mas. Asst)
John Owen (Seaman)

(Lives lost: 250)

Then Lieut. Rooke wrote a further letter to Sir William Parker on 28th:

---

[3] Moses Margoliouth, Nathan Davis and party.

Tunis. Tuesday, December 28th, 1847

Sir,

I returned last night about 12 p.m. from my search for the wreck of HMS Avenger which I am sorry to say has been of no avail.

I reached as near as possible the spot where she struck on Sunday morning and there cruized (sic) about for some time until assured that she had either got off or sunk in the sea on Tuesday, together from the shift of wind having lifted her. I then wished to land and search the Island of Galita for some further signs, but the cowardly Maltese Crew would neither cruize (sic) any more about or go to the Island and all I could say had no effect on them. I could not even get them to run down that I might speak to two Steamers that were to leeward of the Island. On my way back I spoke (to) one of the Tunisian Gun Boats that was assisting and asked her if she would take me to Galita, but she declined, so I was brought back to Tunis against my will without examining Galita. I am happy to learn on my arrival from Sir Thomas Reade that the Pasha and the French Steamer went round the Island and spoke (to) a fishing boat at anchor there; I saw a third Steamer close to the African shore. All the vessels have returned from the search numbering eight or nine. For further particulars from them I must quote Sir Thomas Reade's letter. The cask found I think must have been one that was in the Gun Room. The accounts sent by the horsemen[4] sent to scour the African Coast have not yet come. Everything possible has now been done and I shall now wait here for orders and to be of any further use

---

[4] Moses, Nathan Davis and party.

in showing the exact spot of the wreck, and that you may think fit, Sir, to order. I think this my best plan in the expectation of a Man-of-War Steamer from Malta.

The vessel this goes by is on the point of sailing immediately. Hoping this will meet your approbation.

I have the honour to remain,
Sir, Yours &c.
(Signed) *Lieut. Francis Rooke.*

P.S. I have had every assistance here from the authorities.

A little later, Lieut. Rooke wrote to Sir Lucius Curtis Bt.[5] Although there is inevitable repetition, this dramatic account is worth quoting in full:

On Her Majesty's Ship 'Ceylon'
Malta, 5th January, 1848
Sir,
I beg to lay before you as well as I recollect the proceedings of H.M. Steam-Frigate 'Avenger' from the time of leaving Gibraltar till her wreck.

Friday, 17th December, 1847. The Oriental Mail arriving this afternoon in the 'Pasha' Packet, the 'Avenger' left Gibraltar under steam, an American Frigate weighing the same time, which Captain Napier hailed on passing and offered his services in

---

[5] Sir Lucius Curtis, 2nd Bt. (1786-1869). Admiral of the Fleet and K.C.B. His father, the 1st Baronet, received his title in September, 1794, in consideration of his heroic achievements under Lord Howe in the memorable engagement when the English defeated the French off Ushant at the Battle of the Glorious First of June (1794).

towing her clear of the Rock, which were declined. Weather fine and calm.

Saturday, 18th December. Got a light breeze and as the Captain seemed most anxious to save coal, we made sail and set the Starboard Studding Sails, and the wind being steady (but freshening fast), reduced the steam to the least possible degree, just leaving enough to work the wheels up to our rate of sailing; we did not disconnect owing to some little sea that there was now on. This forenoon we saw the 'Pasha' Packet close into the African shore; also a Brig running outside of us – the wind was increased to a fresh breeze, shortened sail, and before midnight were under double reefed topsails and foresail, the wind being on the Starboard Quarter, and going at the average rate of nine knots an hour.

Sunday, 19th December. Went to Divisions, mustered by open List, read the Articles of War and went to Church – the wind freshened during the night; hooked relieving tackles. The Captain makes the Officers of the Watch call him on all occasions, and I did so four times in my first Watch.

Monday, 20th December. This morning we again observed the 'Pasha' Packet, but soon lost sight of her; excercised (sic) casting loose and securing the guns.

We were now running with the square yard, eight or nine knots steering about E/S under double reefed Topsails and reefed Foresail, and with just steam enough (I think one boiler), to work the wheels up to the time the ship struck.

The weather squally with a good deal of sea on. In the Gun Room we had all been sitting and talking together (except the Master, who was engaged in the Captain's Cabin with Charts), when about 10 o'clock in the First Watch and just as we had retired to our cabins, we were startled by a sudden jerk, which Lieutenant Marrgatt and myself immediately called out was a Gun adrift, but whilst yet speaking she gave a kind of heavy lazy roll, as if filling and having from her impetus gone over, and every beam loosened – we all ran on deck some without coats, myself with a cap, and on our arrival found everybody on, or coming up, and the water they said was rushing in forward. The Captain who was standing on the Paddle Box immediately gave the order 'out with the Boats': this was the only order given, and the last I saw of Captain Napier.

I had seen from the first instant that, (though a poor one), from the sea on at the time, that the Cutters ought immediately to be lowered and lay off the ship; I directly called men to clear them away, casting off the Gripes of the Starboard one myself, when Mr Ottey, Masters Assistant, coming up to me, I told him to make haste and join me in her, on the other side of the ship. Then crossing to the Port Cutter, I met Mr Larcom, the Gunner, coming up half dressed he being in bed when she struck. I ordered him to help me in getting down, and come into the Boat, some more hands assisting. As the Boat touched the water, the ship brought up with a shock, I think from striking another rock.

The sail was on all this time, she swung broadside to the sea, head towards Africa, and fell to windward on her starboard beam ends, with her Deck exposed, Foremast, Mainmast and Mizen Topmast falling over the side, and the Funnel at the same time on the starboard Gangway and the Starboard Paddle Box probably stove, the steam escaping, as I suppose the water put the fires out, the sea was breaking over the forecastle; I pulled away some yards from the Ship, and then kept her head to the sea, with the oars ready to save as many as she would hold, in the event of the ship sinking or breaking up.

The Gig swamped astern and the other Cutter I suppose shared the same fate, as her Breakers were floating about – the moon shining out showed Galita plainly, as I thought bearing N.E. twelve miles. I also saw Africa, but it being cloudy and beginning to rain I only got occasional glimpses. After about an hour and a half, the Boat drawing away from the Ship, and the Crew exhausted, a heavy sea on at the time, I ran before the wind towards Galita, but from it veering round in a severe squall, with Thunder, Lightning, Hail and Rain. I eventually reached the African shore next morning about 10 a.m., the three men and myself being saved in the most extraordinary manner. The Boat upset in the Breakers, by which the other four lost their lives; this was about five miles to the Westward of the Fratellis Rocks; we afterwards made our way across country to Tunis to get assistance for the Ship.

Mr Larcom the Gunner states that about 4 p.m. on Monday the 29th the Master came on Deck and took the bearings of Cape Faro and wrote it on the Log Slate S.W. by W. six leagues.

From statements of Mr Betts, 2nd Master, who was with me in the Boat and Officer of the Watch at the time, on seeing Galita he went down and told the Captain and Master who then came on deck, and were there when she struck, which must have been almost immediately. Her head E. by S. at the time, going about nine knots; he also corroborated Mr Larcom's statement.

Owen a leading Stoker states that he was in the

Stoke hole when she struck, and that Mr Hurst first Engineer directly said 'Stop her and light the other Fires', which Owen said he tried to do, but from the water rushing in he was forced to leave, when he came with me in the boat.

I beg in conclusion to bring prominently before your Notice the Conduct of Mr Larcom, Gunner, from whose cool judgement I have received the greatest possible assistance, both from his management in the Boat, and subsequently whilst seeking assistance for our Ship, and I cannot speak in too high terms of him.

The conduct of Hill (the Captain's Steward) throughout our hardships, merits my approbation. Whole complement: 250 men which I think was full.

(signed) *Lieutenant Francis Rooke*

★

Moses recorded at this time that on his return to Tunis he had 'helped two Jews into the Christian faith.' This took place in Nathan Davis' temporary mission; Mr Davis performed the baptism itself, and Moses read the lesson.'[6] Also to Moses' satisfaction an Italian Roman Catholic, during the baptism service, 'presented himself before the whole congregation requesting to be admitted into the Protestant Church'. This was accepted, and 'I then concluded the service, and preached a sermon suitable to the occasion.' He proudly, and perhaps over-confidently, went on to report that 'these converts... I may safely say, are the first in Tunis since the seventh century'!

This was a tiny drop of good news amidst what had

---

[6] The younger of these two converts – by name Uzan – was to visit Moses in England two years later.

become, almost literally, a sea of troubles. He heard at this time that his friend Felix Mendelssohn[7] (the Queen's favourite composer) had died at a tragically early age, and another matter now arose which further added to both the mental and physical strain he was enduring: he was called upon to attend the bedside of the daughter of the American Consul, Samuel Heap – the same man he had met during the fiesta. The poor girl was mortally ill, and for the last ten days of her life he kept watch over her, 'during which period I scarcely enjoyed ten hours of sleep.'

The cumulative effect of all these matters was to bring him to a state of near-exhaustion. For a time his experiences had ceased to be those of a normal nineteenth century traveller. The drama and tension were proving too big a strain. In his own words, 'I began to feel very unwell. My constitution began to give way very rapidly, so much so that I hardly had strength enough to speak.' In short, he suffered a nervous breakdown, and was advised to return to Malta as soon as possible to seek rest and medical advice. This he did, but not before he had written to England suggesting a reward should be given to the Arab who had so bravely saved Lieut. Rooke and his fellows. The matter came before the House of Lords on 29th February, when Lord Malmesbury enquired whether any recompense had been made. The Earl of Auckland replied that the affair would be attended to as soon as enquiries were complete. In due course, the hero was given four hundred piastres (about twelve pounds) by Her Majesty's Government.

It was towards the end of February, 1848, that Moses, forced to abandon his plans to see more of North Africa,

[7] Mendelssohn was the grandson of Moses Mendelssohn, a man held in high esteem by the Jewish fraternity for his learning and philosophical writings. He was a biblical scholar and an important figure in the Jewish Enlightenment – see also above.

embarked on the *Mariner*, and 'after a delightful sail of three days', he arrived back in Malta to relax and recuperate.

Chapter V
The Pilgrimage: Part Two

Back safely in Malta, he was free from the stress of the past few weeks and, as intended, he could rest and gather strength for the next stage of his journey. He was in need of some good news for a change, and was delighted to hear that the Avenger Court Martial, recently held on board HMS Trafalgar in Malta Harbour, had completely exonerated the four survivors of the shipwreck.[1] The action of Francis Rooke had been declared 'most officer-like and praiseworthy', and that of the Gunner, John Larcom, 'manly and seamanlike'. The Court nevertheless considered it necessary to state that 'the evidence produced leaves a doubt in the mind of the Court as to whether the *Avenger* had on board the usual Mediterranean charts at the time of her wreck'. Moses now went on to consult 'some physicians', and from their advice he 'profited considerably'. He was in no immediate hurry to leave the island, and for a short time he enjoyed the sunshine and relaxing atmosphere of his surroundings. He was soon much recovered.

On 17th March he met a group of Jews who by chance knew the Rabbi from Thessalonica to whom he had given assistance in Liverpool. They said they had 'come under his influence', but whether they had actually become Christians is not recorded. Moses was delighted to have news of his old friend. By an amazing coincidence he was

---

[1] For more details of the Court Martial, see Appendix IV.

soon destined to bump into him, almost literally, during the course of his pilgrimage. Also: 'Whilst at Malta I received a note from a gentleman – a Mr Woodcock of Leicestershire[2] – who was on his way to the Holy Land. He asked me whether I would have any objection to accept him as a fellow-traveller so that he might join me in my pilgrimage. From his note and his manner I could have no objection.' As a result the two teamed up and remained together for the rest of the journey. The arrangement was to prove helpful and added much to Moses' enjoyment over the next few months. From time to time there is no doubt that he found Mr Woodcock irritating; they didn't agree on every matter, but they generally did get on well and were able jointly to make plans regarding travel and accommodation, and problems when they arose could be shared.

By mid-March they had both embarked on the 'Erin' from Valetta, and before the end of the month they entered harbour in Constantinople (Istanbul). Early on the morning of the day they arrived, the Captain – Captain Russell – knocked on Moses' cabin door suggesting he should come on deck to enjoy the fine panoramic view of the city and its famous outline of temples, mosques and palaces. He was enthralled and, as usual, could hardy wait to inspect his new surroundings. He and Mr Woodcock at once set off on their tour of the city, and saw the Sultan ('with whose appearance I was by no means struck') on his way to prayer. They sailed up the Bosphorus and into the Black Sea. He was much impressed: 'I am inclined to think that there is scarcely another spot in the whole globe equal to it in

---

[2] In 1850 M.M. noted: 'Mr Woodcock has since taken Holy Orders, and is now at St Agnes, Nassau, New Providence. He has published an interesting little volume on Palestine, bearing the title *Scripture Lands: being a visit to the scenes of the Bible*. Their relationship remained a formal one. Moses always referred to him as Mr Woodcock. His Christian name is unknown.

beauty.'

They stayed at Misseri's Hotel, and from there he wrote to his father giving a lively description of the city, significantly with emphasis on its importance in world trade. He also couldn't resist telling him: 'The Sultan I hear is beginning to be Europeanised: he has introduced an Italian dancing-master into the seraglio.' He described the beauty of the St Sophia Mosque and the palace of King Emanuel: 'The Greeks who inhabit the country are extremely rich and possess great wealth of gold and precious stones.'

Moses and his friend looked round many 'churches, mosques, synagogues and coffee houses.' He noted that in the latter was much talk of the latest French Revolution.[3] The 1840s was an exciting time to travel round Europe. The new and ever-expanding railway system facilitated movement, and there was a corresponding expansion in mercantile and passenger shipping in which Liverpool was playing its part. But there was also at this time an element of danger. England was politically and constitutionally tranquil, but in other parts of Europe democrats and nationalists were restive and showing their teeth. Every day newspapers brought news of an uprising or a dethronement. An example of this was the House of Orleans whose overthrow had caused Louis Phillippe to seek refuge in England. Moses saw first hand evidence of this almost as soon as he arrived in Turkey. One day he heard shouts of 'Vive la Republique' and witnessed an angry crowd threatening the French Embassy – so much so that 'the poor

---

[3] France was one of those countries in turmoil at this time. Louis-Philippe, known as the 'Citizen King', ruled France from 1830 to 1848. Political corruption and economic depression led to unrest and ultimately to his overthrow in February, 1848. Over the following few weeks the echoes of the Revolution resounded round the capitals of the world, and Moses was in Constantinople just when its effects were apparent there.

ambassador, an out and out aristocrat, was apprehensive of his ultimate safety.[4]

For the first time in over ten years he had the opportunity to speak Russian – 'it was quite refreshing to me to have a chat in the Russian language after my tongue has been dumb to it for so long.' There were many Russian soldiers in the city and their presence was in fact an ominous sign; there was talk of an invasion, and the Golden Horn was 'at present paraded with Turkish frigates, and cannons are constantly fired.' The Crimean war was not far away.

In the city were about five hundred Russian and Polish pilgrims on their way to Jerusalem. He met an old Jewess aged eighty who was determined to reach the land of her fathers in order to die there. On March 21st he went by boat to Hass Kieu, the Jewish quarter. He had chosen a bad day because the funeral of a well known Rabbi was taking place, and the throng was so great that his boat was delayed for over an hour. He watched the goings-on for some time and then re-crossed the Golden Horn to visit Balat, and inspect the synagogues there in the company of a guide. As is known from the Ferriere portrait, Moses was clean-shaven but a fellow-Jew there told him he should be wearing a beard. His guide promptly came to his aid by saying he'd rather have a good Jew without a beard than a

---

[4] The aristocrat to whom Moses referred was François-Adolphe, Baron and Comte of Bourqueney, Special Envoy and Minister Plenipotentiary to Turkey from 1841. In his despatches sent to the Department on the day after the February Revolution, and following his dismissal (eventually confirmed on 15th July), he made no mention of this episode. On the other hand, Mathurin-Joseph Cor, a senior official at the Embassy, who became Chargé d'Affaires in March, pointed out in his letter of the 27th March that the demonstration by his fellow citizens was sufficiently alarming as to cause the Turkish authorities to call for French Government assistance and in response more than three hundred French nationals were summoned to give protection.

beard without a good Jew!

The following day he continued to look at what he called 'the lions' – i.e. the tourist sights. He once again visited the St Sophia Mosque which he noted was under repair, and spent some time in the main Jewish bookshop. Whenever possible he put the case for Christianity to his fellow Jews while continuing his exploration of the Jewish quarter. Amongst the many religious buildings he saw, he considered the Caraite synagogue quite 'the nicest of all'. Inside he found several Hebrew bibles published by the Bible Society, and the Jews there 'kindly allowed me to take a roll of the law from its sanctum, which I unfolded and preached the Gospel to those present.'

On the 27th, the day before he and Mr Woodcock set sail again, he went round the Sultan's Medical School. He was pleased to see that the principal was a Jew, and there were twenty-four Jewish students, for whom the Sultan magnanimously granted leave of absence every Saturday. This was Moses' and Mr Woodcock's last day in Constantinople, and they were to look back on their several days in Turkey as amongst the most memorable of their lives. On their last night they slept well, and the following morning they both boarded the 'Stamboul', and set sail for Rhodes, Cyprus and Beyrout (Beirut). To their dismay the boat was more crowded than any vessel they had experienced. By now they had picked up two more companions – a Mr Stone, 'a young English officer who had sold out,' and a Dutchman, Mr Hooglandt, from Amsterdam. To Moses annoyance, Mr Woodcock had immediately secured for himself a separate berth, and Messrs. S. and H. (as he called them) shared a berth, while Moses had to make do with 'a sofa in the large saloon.'

There were many Jews on board, including the old lady hoping to end her life in Jerusalem – Moses doubted whether she'd make it! As they sailed away he 'stood and gazed in the same direction till ten o'clock in the evening, and the image of my last view of Constantinople continues dazzling me.'

Their first stop was Smyrna (Izmir), where, to the Captain's annoyance, many would-be guides clambered on board to offer their services. Amid the confusion, Moses and Mr Woodcock managed to select one who said he would show them round and be, as they thought, their 'trumpeter'. They agreed to take him on but on the strict condition that he wouldn't blow his trumpet. On these terms they disembarked and were met on the quayside by Mr Solbe, who was the missionary there working under the auspices of the London Society for Promoting Christianity among Jews. One of their first excursions was to be taken by the guide round one of the many bazaars in the town, and through the guide Mr Woodcock enquired the price of an item of clothing which had taken his fancy. They were amazed when the guide flatly refused to help, on the grounds that it was contrary to their agreement. Much to their amusement Mr Solbe later discovered that when he said he would be their 'trumpeter', he had really said 'interpreter'!

On 31st March they sailed on to Rhodes and from there to Larnaca, Cyprus. Moses had specifically promised Lady Powerscourt, one of his Dublin friends, that he would write from Cyprus, so he was definitely now on a section of his journey which was pre-arranged.[5] It was a Sunday, and he had decided to remain all day on board. He explained that he had conducted a short service for all the Protestants on the ship, but in the middle of the proceedings they were interrupted by the harem of a Turk who was making for Beyrout. 'The whole tribe appeared, some yashmaked, and

[5] Sadly Lady Powerscourt died on 5th April before receiving Moses' letter. She was the widow of the 4th Viscount.

88

others yet unveiled, to see what was going on.' It was like a scene from a musical comedy. He went on, 'They made such a clatter and set up such laughing that I was obliged to threaten that I would send for their husband'. They immediately rushed headlong back to their quarters, and the service was recommenced. 'But,' he said, 'by degrees they came out one by one from their shell to favour us with a second edition of their merriment.' One final threat that the whole matter would be reported to their husband at last did the trick and 'we enjoyed peace during the remainder of our worship.' A Greek Patriarch was more polite – he made enquiries about their liturgy, and a group of Jews also asked to hear a few more prayers, and he lent them a copy of the Book of Common Prayer in Hebrew.

Also on board he met a young Pole who turned out to be from Suwalki, the son of a neighbour. He told Moses that his whole family had become converted to Christianity, and his late father had often expressed a wish 'to be permitted to see the son of Gershon Margoliouth who became a member of the Christian Church.' He particularly queried why Moses spent so much time with his Jewish brethren after his conversion. Moses said, 'I preached the poor fellow a regular sermon and pointed out to him the mischief which professing Christendom has done to the cause of Christ by persecuting the Jews'.

He received a letter at this time from Dr August Neander[6] of Berlin asking whether he ever heard from 'Apollyon Napoleon' since leaving Ireland. This odd title referred to the Archbishop of Dublin who had written a highly controversial pamphlet entitled 'The Historic

[6] Johann August Wilhelm Neander 1789–1850. German Protestant church historian and theologian. Of Jewish parentage. Was pupil of Schleiermacher. Embraced Christianity 1806. Professor of church history, Berlin, from 1813. Moses greatly admired him.

Doubts with reference to Napoleon Bonaparte.[7] Moses replied, 'As I have left Dublin I suppose he no more feels any interest in my movements.' His Grace had never been Moses' favourite prelate. He went on to tell Dr Neander that they stopped for a few hours at Rhodes – 'an advantage over St Paul,' he said, 'who just sailed past.' He particularly remarked on the beauty of Rhodes, and was reluctant to leave.

The following day, the 2nd April, they were in Larnaca and the British Consul there asked Moses if he would Christen his small son, which he did at two o'clock in the afternoon of the 3rd.[8]

It was then a short sail to the mainland, and on 4th April he first set eyes on 'the scriptural and glorious Lebanon.' On docking, his party was bothered with 'soliciting cicerones, corrupt custom-house officers, and exhorting Arab boatmen and porters,' but nevertheless he couldn't forget that he was treading on the 'Land of Promise.'

He was quite overcome with emotion as he and his

---

[7] This oddity was published in 1819. Richard Whateley (1787–1863) was Archbishop of Dublin from 1831 up to his death. His caustic wit and outspokenness made him unpopular. He was born in London; was a Fellow of Oriel College, Oxford, 1811–12, M.A. 1812 and D.D. 1825. He edited an anti-Calvinistic treatise on predestination in 1821, and was Drummond Professor of political economy 1829-31. Arriving in Dublin on his appointment as Archbishop he founded a chair of political economics at TCD in 1832. He was a founder-member of the Broad Church Party. Moses clearly didn't care for him and the feeling was no doubt mutual. It is unlikely that the 'upstart' Margoliouth was to the Archbishop's taste; Moses was an intellectual match for him. Moses' mercurial mind must have jarred on that of his superior. Neither can Bishop Lindsay's patronage of his young protégé have met with the Archbishop's approval.

[8] The name of the British Consul in Larnaca at this period was Niven Kerr. He was appointed in April, 1843 and from Cyprus was transferred to Rhodes in 1849, which post he held until 1853, when he was exchanged to Dunkirk.

friends stepped ashore, and he needed some time to gather
his thoughts before deciding on his next move. Their
immediate requirement was suitable accommodation, and
this they found in a hotel about half a mile from the town
centre. It catered for the European trade and was kept by a
Maltese called Antonio. He met there Lord Berisford[9], and
Mr Richard Brooke.[10] Moses remarked that Mr Brooke was
a person of 'very good taste and sound common sense'. He
also met a Mr Winbolt or, as he described him, 'poor Mr
Winbolt'. He was the Protestant clergyman in Beyrout, and
had an uphill battle in his attempts to spread the Gospel
there. He appeared to be delicate, and although every day
he took a service in the town, very few attended. Moses felt
sorry for him and considered his task needed someone with
a stronger personality and constitution.

On the Saturday he inevitably visited the synagogue. He
was welcomed by the Rabbi who apologised for the
behaviour of the women who sat upstairs and chattered
noisily during the service; they were ill-educated and knew
no better. Moses was asked to dine later at the Rabbi's
house, and a number of his fellow-guests had been passengers on the *Stamboul*.

On another evening he went to a dinner party given by
Colonel Rose, the British Consul-General. There he met a
Mr Lowthian of Carleton House, near Carlisle, who was
trying out English methods of agriculture in that area, but
with little success.

The time soon came to set out on their overland trek to
Jerusalem, first making for Damascus. Mr Woodcock was
of course still with him, and they had also added Messrs. S.
and H. to their party. They each paid twenty francs a day to

---

[9] 3rd Marquess of Waterford. 1811–1859.
[10] Son of Sir Richard Brooke of Norton Priory, Runcorn, Cheshire. This
Richard Brooke, born 1814, succeeded his father as the 7th baronet in
1865 and died in 1888.

a couple of Christian Arab guides who, for the price, included tents, mules, muleteers and food. They further agreed between them that if they came to a place of any size, this would cover hotel accommodation, and it would be the responsibility of the guides to settle up with the innkeeper. Moses noted, 'You may travel comfortably for one pound per day in this manner in Palestine.'

The packing, preparation and arranging took six hours, and they eventually said goodbye to Antonio and set out, looking, Moses said, 'rather consequential'. Their group consisted of four pilgrims, two guides and four muleteers. From the hill outside the town they stood for a time looking back in silence at the view: 'it is beautiful and charming – the mulberry trees, olive trees, vines, apricots, cypresses, interspersed with minarets and cupolas, and the unfurled flag-staffs of the various consulates giving the city an imposing character.' They now turned south-east, Moses feeling full of emotion, and regretting that he had no brother-Jew with whom he could share his feelings; 'Mr Woodcock is a good and pious man, but cannot feel the same in his breast'.

It was tough going from the start due to the condition of the roads. 'I am sure no English horses, unless purposely trained, could ever pass by such paths as those we took that evening.' They eventually arrived at a place called Khan Kashan, where they camped for the night. It was pictur-esque, but the village was nothing but 'a miserable collection of little huts.' Nearby, an Arab chief had also set up camp, travelling with his 'wives, eunuchs, pipe-bearers and servants.' The women came to inspect Moses and his party, and Mr Stone 'wondered whether the chief would part with any of his conjugal stock!'

They now decided to make for the famous ruins at

Baalbeck,[11] travelling via the Bekka valley. This was perhaps a last-minute change of plan because it forced them to go north, taking them quite some distance out of their way. Moses had become determined to visit the celebrated and sensational ruins of the huge Roman temple there. It was reputed to have taken no less than two hundred and fifty years to build, and Moses justifiably described it as 'one of the great wonders of the world'. When they at last arrived after a strenuous nine-hour journey, he wrote: 'The ruined majesty completely overcame me; I could do nothing else but creep and climb from one apartment to the other, gaze, examine, admire and say nothing – I slowly rode round and round the temple, gazing all the time at the beautiful, grand and mysterious structure. The first sight one catches of the great ruin gives the idea of a petrified forest of palm trees.' Moses was in raptures with it all, and certainly thought the detour more than well worth while, and his companions, in spite of earlier grumbles, felt they had to agree. Then, having taken their fill of the sights of Baalbeck, they turned south to resume their travels.

The following day they arrived at Damascus, where Moses met a Rabbi who showed him an ancient and celebrated manuscript of the Pentateuch, dating from the sixth century: 'He, (the Rabbi) took out an antiquated and elaborately worked wooden box which he opened and produced a large silver box, fantastically chased, out of which he took a beautifully worked silk wrapper, which he unfolded, and out came a gorgeous, unrivalled, truly unique triumph of penmanship.' He later told his companions about it, and Mr Woodcock and Mr Brooke insisted on being taken to see it. (It is interesting that Mr Brooke was with them still, but apparently he soon goes his own way.)

---

[11] It has recently become more accessible, but for many years was a 'well-kept secret', being off the tourist maps.

Moses also met in Damascus the well known Farhi family; they lived there in great style, and their mansion was 'splendid and grand'. They had a mutual friend, a Mr Pieritz, who was a missionary with the Society for Propagating the Gospel in Foreign Parts, and this proved as useful as a letter of introduction. Moses and his friends were staying at the Hotel de l'Europe, where he met the wife of a Polish Rabbi who was very outspoken: she knew of his family and all about Moses' conversion, and she 'lamented the curse which I inflicted on my family'.[12]

At this time Moses was becoming more and more anxious to reach Jerusalem. He had heard a rumour that the Protestant church there was to be consecrated within a day or two, and he was very keen to be present at this ceremony if at all possible. It was still April, and he was putting his whole party under pressure to speed up the final stage of their pilgrimage. They passed through Safet (Safad), and were soon in Nazareth, from where he wrote: 'I will not trouble you with the reflections which filled my mind. You can easily imagine the feeling of a Christian on a Lord's day for the first time in the place where the Saviour of the World tabernacled.'

But he was still anxious to press on, and when his friends out-voted him ('they said they did not come to Palestine with the express purpose of killing themselves!'), he decided that he just could not wait; he would take one of the guides and leave the rest to make it in their own time. There was some argument: 'It was objected to on the grounds that I should be sure to be murdered,' and it was indeed true that there was bound to be safety in numbers, but he would have none of it. It would be, said his friend Mr Woodcock, a plain case of suicide. At 5 a.m., in the

---

[12] It is surely to his credit that Moses was prepared to put this incident on record.

company of a nervous guide, Saloom, he set off for Jerusalem.

After about half-an-hour's ride, they met an egg-seller at the side of the road who, with threats, tried to make a sale. Moses said he would count out a quantity into the Arab's lap and then decide. When he was sufficiently loaded, they leaped into their saddles and left the salesman cursing and shouting with 'vehement cordiality!'

Their next stop was Sebasta, where they inspected the 'noble columns', and then straight on to Nablous where they rested for a few hours in the 'house of a Christian'. With his usual enthusiasm he visited the Jewish quarter and looked round the Samaritan synagogues. It was here in Nablous that he bought, at some considerable expense, an amulet (see later). It was the eve of the Passover, and he witnessed the Sacrifice of the Paschal Lamb on Mount Gerizim. There he preached for an hour in the synagogue and reported that he was 'listened to with undivided attention!' Then, at midnight, he and the faithful Saloom set off to cover the last thirty-five miles to Jerusalem.

As if in a dream he arrived in Jerusalem the following day after travelling all night. Hardly pausing for breath, he went at once to see the Bishop of Jerusalem, the Rt. Revd Samuel Gobat[13] and his wife, who received their weary and travel-stained visitor with cordiality and no doubt a degree of incredulity. Moses at once took to them – he found them both charming and, as for the Bishop, 'he seems a delightful character, a true apostolical one.' He also recorded: 'The next person I paid a visit to was my dear friend the Revd F.C. Ewald[14] for whom I have a sincere regard, and so must

[13] Bishop Samuel Gobat of Jerusalem was born 26 January 1799 and died 11 May 1879. He was a Prussian Lutheran.

[14] Christian Ferdinand Ewald (Note: Moses had his initials reversed.) 1802–1874. Missionary; took Anglican Orders, 1836; laboured in

everyone who knows him thoroughly.' He then explored the east side of the city, going through St Stephen's Gate. 'I descended the rough eastern declivity of Mount Moriah, gazed for a time upon the blocked-up Golden Gate, passed over a bridge across the Valley of Kedron, ran in for a few moments to the Garden of Gethsemane.' He was extremely moved by the whole experience, and he then turned and re-entered the city, 'descending the Mount of Olives.' He then wrote: 'And now I am almost exhausted, unfit for anything else considering I did not sleep a wink the whole of last night. Good night.'

He must have slept like a log. The following day, refreshed, he continued his exploration of Jerusalem, visiting a number of synagogues where he recognised and met several fellow-passengers from the boat. He was much upset by the Arab occupation of the city ('the beauty of our land belongs now to strangers, our strength to aliens...'), but he was pleased to acknowledge that the Jews had their own quarter without restriction. It was Easter week and there was an Anglican service each morning at 11 a.m. One day near to the Protestant church (it was what he described as a 'temporary chapel'), he saw a figure he seemed to recognise. To his astonishment it was none other than his old friend the Rabbi from Thessalonica whom he had last seen in Liverpool five years before. Moses was with his friend Mr Ewald at the time, and at first he was speechless. To add to the drama of the situation the Rabbi told him that he was about to be baptised into the Christian church, there in Jerusalem, on Good Friday! It was on that day in 1838 that Moses himself had been baptised in Liverpool, and here he was, destined to be a witness at that ceremony for his Greek friend – Rabbi Shuffami. Moses at once wrote

Jerusalem for the London Society for Propagating the Gospel among the Jews, from 1841. (*Webster's Biographical Dictionary*).

Nineteenth-century print: Carthage in its declining years from the painting by J M W Turner.

Nineteenth-century print: The Mount of Olives from Jerusalem.

to Revd Joseph to tell him, recording the Greek's 'solemn aspect', and recounting that there was 'a cluster of wondering and displeased Jews who stood near the door', and he told of 'the deep solemn tone of the baptismal service... which gave a primitive and apostolic character to the first religious service I was present at on Mount Zion.' Unusually, he later attended a Roman Catholic service – the Latin Festival of the Crucifixion, in the Church of the Holy Sepulchre which, predictably, he didn't enjoy. Then, later still, he visited the chapel of the Greek church, which he found deeply impressive.

Starting with this astonishing coincidence, Moses' momentous time in Jerusalem, the climax of his long journey, was a highlight in his life. He wrote, he said, hundreds of letters at this time to England and Poland, and no doubt they meant more to his father than words could express. For Gershon, the land of his fathers was being depicted in a series of descriptive essays which were avidly read and re-read, and proudly shown to the rest of the family and to friends in Suwalki. Assuming that Gershon was defraying the cost of it all, the reward of letters was ample recompense for the rich store of information which was relayed back to him.

On Easter Day he attended the Protestant Chapel, the service being taken by Bishop Gobat. He told Miriam that the Bishop and his wife were delightful – 'just such persons as a bishop and bishopess should be'. The following Sunday, at the Bishop's request, he preached a sermon, which he considered a great privilege. Most of the days he spent walking round, examining the buildings and talking to the inhabitants. Mr Woodcock, Mr Stone and Mr Hooglandt had by now caught up with him in Jerusalem, but it seems that for the time being they were obviously pursuing their own ways, and presumably the guide, muleteers and mules had all been sent home. Moses' most frequent walk was 'to leave the city by the Jaffa Gate which is on Mount Zion, towards the west; from thence I descend into the lower Pool of Gihon, and then ramble for some time on the southern part of Mount Zion, which is literally ploughed as a field. It is now crowned with waving corn from which I plucked a few ears and prize them like so many sacred relics. I sit there many an hour gazing on the scenery before me, and musing over the mighty events that happened there in days of Yore.'

One day he went early to the market area so that he could report to his father on the system of wholesale and retail in the fruit and vegetable trade (a strong indication that this was Gershon's line of business.) The stallholders, in from the countryside (from Bethlehem, Betshaan, Ainhereen, etc), would sell only to shopkeepers – no retail trade took place at this time in the morning. The goods were bought by the sack or box, and the deal struck after much shouting and bargaining; the whole process was finished and the market square cleared by 9 a.m. By then the shops would be open and ready for the general public.

On 12th May a small group, now including Mr Woodcock again, set out for Hebron. They left by the Jaffa Gate, crossed the Valley of Hinnon by means of the raised pathway at the head of the Pool of Gihon; ascending the opposite hill, they crossed the Plain of Rephaim. After a journey of six and a half hours the party reached 'the ancient city of Hebron, one of the four holy cities of the Jews.' Interesting for Moses, they attended a service there in a Polish synagogue. The next day, Sunday 14th, they all went to a Church of England service in a room kindly lent to them for the purpose in the Jewish Mission House, at which Moses preached on the text Deut. 4:9–10.[15] After-

---

[15] Only take heed to thyself, and keep thy soul diligently, lest thou forget the things which thine eyes have seen, and lest they depart from thy heart all the days of thy life: but teach them thy sons, and thy sons' sons;

wards they were shown round a new quarantine hospital, not quite finished – their guide, a French doctor, 'very civil'. On the Monday they made the return journey back to Jerusalem.

Another excursion was to the Plain of Jericho – again, a long day's trip. From there he wrote a letter to the Josephs which reveals something of his character. It is playfully headed, 'Jericho, tent, May 1848,' and goes on: 'I suppose you will be delighted with yourself on the receipt of this. You will say 'serve the little fellow right; he should not have teazed (sic) and tormented me so much and I would not have wished him at Jericho!' (He was at this time planning his return to England as he suggested that Mr Joseph should write to him c/o Revd, Wm. Hare, 3 Strada St Paolo, Malta). Another self-revelatory remark at this point: he found an old mother-of-pearl ring in the mud by the river Jordan. There were some women standing nearby, and his friends pulled his leg on the subject. Of this incident, he wrote: 'Little do they know my feelings on that subject. Oh no!' These few words reveal much.

Soon after this he spent several days camping on the north side of the Dead Sea. He was very much in the right place at the right time because his presence coincided with an American expedition investigating that area, and he had long discussions with Capt. Lynch, the expedition leader. On seeing the American flag raised, he commented, 'it is waving its stars upon the Dead Sea; so that the United States are extending their union even to Almotana!'[16]

A further notable trip which he and Mr Woodcock

Specially the day that thou stoodest before the LORD thy God in Horeb, when the LORD said unto me, Gather me the people together, and I will make them hear my words, that they may learn to fear me all the days that they shall live upon the earth, and *that* they may teach their children. (Authorised Version).

[16] Almotana was one of the oriental terms for the Dead Sea.

undertook in May was to the Caves of Adullam.[17] They had collected together a party comprising a total of eight, which involved extra responsibility as two of their number were women. With them were a Mr and Mrs Simeon, a Mr and Mrs Bergheim, a Mr Synianki and a Mr Calman. They had been advised to take Lucifer matches, wax candles and plenty of string.

They made their way again, due south, to Bethlehem, and from there, each on horseback, they rode to the caves. It was a difficult journey: 'Many were the rugged mountains which lay in our road; some of them were precipitous, and consisting by no means of terra firma.' Adullam was 'one of the oldest cities of the Caananites', and 'bearing many marks of high antiquity.' Moses gave Lady Mary Lindsay an account of the visit: 'We had to make our way by a slanting edge of rock, of about three feet in width, projecting from the middle of the rock. As you are aware that I am not very headstrong, I soon became giddy, and was on the point of precipitation, but thanks to Mr Bergheim's helping hand I at last reached two isolated pieces of rock, one above the other, of about twenty feet in height, which I had to climb up; at the top of which I discovered a chasm of several feet in width, and not being an expert leaper, I condescended to descend first into the

---

[17] An interesting curiosity: the expression 'Cave of Adullam' entered the political vocabulary in 1866. Most Liberals supported the Government's 1866 Reform Bill, but there were one or two antagonistic, particularly Messrs Lowe and Horsman. John Bright, referring to Horsman, said in the Houses of Commons: 'The hon. gentleman had retired into what he called his political Cave of Adullam, to which he invited every one who was in distress, and every one who was discontented.' (with the Bill). Several others joined the original two in the 'Cave', and the failure of the Bill caused the fall of the Government. This in turn led to the Hyde Park riots in July of that year. Judge Edmond Beales (1803–1881) was president of the Reform League at the time of the riots. The judge was a friend of Moses (see later).

hole and then climb up the other side. At last, as instructed, we lighted our candles, took hold the string, and proceeded farther and farther into that wonderful cavern. It is an astounding production of nature, or rather of nature's God. Sometimes we had to crawl on all fours for ten yards together and then found ourselves in a spacious, extensive, lofty and magnificent apartment, supported by columns almost of Corinthian architecture; at the other end of which a number of holes appeared for our selection. We chose one and crawled again, and once more rose in a vaulted chamber of extraordinary altitude; fit, if illuminated, for the abode, not only for a prince in exile, but for a monarch in the meridian of glory. It would take many days fully to explore the labyrinth of the cavework system. The only way to find one's way out again is to have secured the string at the mouth of the cave and to go no farther than the string would allow.'

He reckoned that they were at one point about seven hundred yards from the cave mouth. 'The reflection of the lighted candles on their snow-white walls lends a bewitching splendour to the dark abode. The echo of 'where are you?' bounded from vault to vault, from passage to passage, as if from a multitude of departed spirits thus welcoming me to their region of perpetual darkness.' Mr Calman, Moses said, made sure everyone made their way safely outside – 'with all his eccentricities, he is a worthy man.' Once outside, they were greeted by a tremendous storm which added to the theatricality of the experience. 'The effect of the thunder peals and lightning was grand and sublime on the magnificent landscape; the valley was now lit up, the mountains quaking and resounding from a thousand quarters was a scene never to be forgotten.'

It was a grand and dramatic climax to his pilgrimage, as the time was fast approaching for him to leave for England. On 22nd May he wrote to Miriam saying he was planning and packing for the return trip. He spent his last evening in Jerusalem with 'the beloved Bishop's family' – his friendship with the Gobats had become particularly close. His experiences had often been exhausting, exciting and at times sensational. He was now sailing back to reality, and the daily tasks, albeit rewarding and inspiring, of a country curate. A small Cheshire village would be a far cry from the colour and exoticism of Tunis, Constantinople and Jerusalem.

The Synagogue courtyard, Suwalki.
Reproduced with permission from *Landsmen,* the quarterly publication of the
Suwalk-Lomeza Interest Group for Jewish Genealogists, Washington, DC.

St Leonard's Church, Little Linford, Buckinghamshire. Moses was
vicar here for the last four years of his life, 1877-1881.

Wybunbury Church interior, c.1890. This is the church Moses knew during his curacy there, 1853-1855. Demolished 1892, the tower still survives.

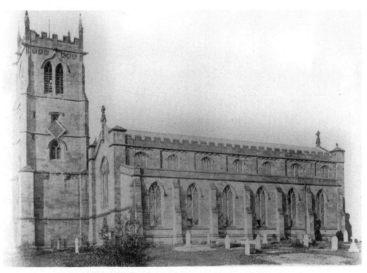

Wybunbury Church exterior c.1890.

East window in Little Linford Church. In memory of Moses Margoliouth.

Little Linford Church and grave of Moses and Sarah Margoliouth.

Photograph of No.3, Rue de Birague, Paris, home of the Goldbergs.

Chapter VI
Back Home

The exact route of his return journey is not known but presumably the ship called at Malta where, as arranged, he picked up correspondence. Liverpool was his destination, and there, for a few months, he again earned his living by teaching.

Early in 1849 he obtained the post of curate in the parish of St Catherine Tranmere situated on the Wirral Peninsular in Cheshire, serving under the Revd Benedict Arthure MA. Both church and parish were fairly new having recently been carved out of the old parish of Bebington and Moses immediately became involved in what was generally considered an urgent need – the building of yet another new church in Limekiln Lane, and the inevitable problems of fund-raising. The intention of those concerned was that he should then be offered the living of this new Tranmere parish to cope with the ever-expanding population of which prosperous and expanding Liverpool was the core. Tranmere village, as it was then, was indeed not far from his old hunting ground, Liverpool – just across the river Mersey – and it is likely that he obtained the position through the recommendation and influence of his old friend Henry Joseph. He was certainly taking services there in March 1849, and his last Christening in St Catherine's was on 22nd September, 1850.

As always, arriving in a new environment, he soon found himself surrounded by a group of new friends. One of these, W. Waring Perrey of Bay House, was one of the parish's more prominent inhabitants. There were already signs that the tranquillity of the area was being disturbed by its proximity to Liverpool. Visiting trouble-makers would come across the Mersey estuary and 'invade' sleepy Tranmere at weekends, and especially during Liverpool Wakes' week. Mr Perrey had approached the local magistracy on several occasions, requesting them to deal more effectively with the marauders, and there were attempts by the Bench to make examples of some of these unwelcome visitors. Moses agreed with his friend, and they also had other interests in common and would meet to discuss many topics, historical and antiquarian, and often Moses would recount details, still fresh in his mind, of his recent adventures around the Mediterranean. Mr Perrey was one of the founder-members of the Lancashire and Cheshire Historical Society.

For most of the time that Moses served at St Catherine's, he lived in Greenway Terrace, a row of early nineteenth century houses, sadly long since gone. Each property had a small garden front and back, and they were situated on Greenway Road, on the corner of Elm Road. They were comfortable, and had sufficient accommodation to include a 'house servant'. His neighbours on one side were the Reeves family (Robert Reeves was a wine merchant, born in Middlewich) and on the other side was, coincidentally, a Jewish family, originally from Manchester; Esther Atalmark, a widow, with her children, John, Job and Joseph. But the family who became particularly close to Moses at this time were the Ashtons. Charles and Sarah Ashton lived at Tranmere Lodge in Church Road. They had four daughters and a son; Charles, the head of the house, worked as a clerk in Her Majesty's Mailing Depot in Liverpool. They showed great kindness to Moses and, perhaps, especially to Miriam and Charles, who had the fortune to be able to play and associate with the Ashton offspring. Charity is not exclusive to Christianity, but there is no doubt that the Ashtons showed remarkable benevolence and hospitality to Moses and his family which is worthy of special record in this narrative.

Unhappily, the relationship between vicar and curate deteriorated during the summer months of 1850. Two matters occurred which became the subject of petty controversy, until at last Moses appealed to the Chancellor of the diocese, Henry Raikes, for assistance. Chancellor Raikes and the two men met on 30th October, at the house of the Revd A. Knox of Birkenhead, and their discussions resulted in the following letter sent by Chancellor Raikes on the same day to each of the two protagonists:

Revd and dear Sirs,

I feel bound to express my gratitude to you for the honour which you conferred, by submitting the case to my consideration, and still more for the manner in which you have conducted the long and anxious inquiry this morning. I rejoice to think that the result has been the complete vindication of Mr Margoliouth's character, and such an alteration of your views towards each other as will enable you to part in a very different frame of mind from that which existed previous to this explanation. There are two cases which required my attention; the first was one where Mr Margoliouth had induced a gentleman to advance the sum of ten pounds on loan to a converted Jew, of whose character he thought so highly, that he did not hesitate to urge the loan, for the purpose of setting him up in business, with the assurance that it would be repaid. The money was not repaid; but it appears that sickness in the family, and want of bread, had caused the misapplication of the loan; and all that can be charged against Mr Margoliouth is want of consideration of the circumstances, and a too confident hope that the first efforts of his countryman would be successful.

In another instance, Mr Margoliouth had received subscriptions to the amount of £10. 5s., for the proposed church in Limekiln Lane, and was supposed to have delayed accounting for them. It appears that this supposition arose from error, and that he merely withheld the payment for the purpose of ascertaining the precise object to which the subscribers intended to apply their contributions. In all these matters of a pecuniary nature, Mr Margoliouth appears free from every shadow of suspicion; and I cannot doubt that Mr Arthure's candour will lead him to take the earliest steps for giving publicity to this statement, and of contradicting any reports of a contrary nature.

A separation has now taken place, and I trust that nothing will be remembered that can prolong the feelings of resentment.

Very faithfully and truly yours,
H. Raikes

So it was that this affair led to Moses' resignation and departure. Tranmere was a mark of his reputation and calibre. He was asked to go there, build a new church and become its first priest. This did not happen because, not for the first or last time, he encountered jealousy and prejudice. At such moments in his life Moses demonstrated optimism and determinism which were almost heroic.

Where was Moses' wife at this time? Had she, with glistening eyes, an excited child in each hand, greeted him on the quayside at Liverpool when he returned from his pilgrimage? It brings to mind an oil painting of the

Victorian school so fashionable now.

This is a possibility. Had she, in 1843, embraced Christianity and produced for Moses a son, later regretting having incurred the wrath and enmity of the Goldberg clan? It is known that Moses often asked his father for information as to the state of the Jewish Nation in Poland. He was of course really wanting to know what it was like to be a Jew over there; by all accounts the future seemed, if not actually grim, certainly ominous, and the Goldbergs, Chaja's parents and brothers, had also joined the Jewish exodus from Poland and were living in Paris. Chaja was surely only too relieved to be away from Poland in 1843, but did she come to the conclusion, during Moses' Tranmere days, that she had had enough of rejection by her family; enough of England and her husband and even her children? The exact circumstances are just not known. The plot has all the Victorian mystery of a Wilkie Collins novel. Certainly, when Moses ended his appointment at St Catherine's, he remained in the parish and stayed for a short time with the Ashtons. There, in comfort, he was able to study and write, and plan his next move. As he had promised his father, he set about assembling for publication some of the many letters he had written whilst on his pilgrimage, and this was issued, in two volumes, in 1850.

It was a busy time for him, because also on his mind at this period was the completion of what was to be his much acclaimed *History of the Jews in Great Britain*, which was published by Richard Bentley of New Burlington Street in the following year. At the time that Miriam and Charles were safely with the Ashtons in Tranmere, Moses was in London making final arrangements for the printing and publication of this three-volume work. It deals with the pre-Conquest period as well as their early training and background as a wandering nation. He takes the reader through the mediaeval and later period, coming up-to-date with an account of the then recent building of a synagogue in Ramsgate, the entire cost of which was borne by Sir Moses and Lady Montefiore, for whom he had high regard. He also couldn't resist telling the story of one Benjamin Benjamin, a wealthy Jewish broker of London who had been in Lincolnshire attending the three-week long auction sale of the possessions of the late Mr C. Mainwaring of Coleby. Lot No. 3122 and the following nine lots, including an antique Spanish mahogany altar table, had been the subject of much controversy as Mr Mainwaring had intended giving them to Hackthorne Church, but had failed to specify this in his will. When the first of this series of lots came up, Mr Benjamin rose to announce that he would offer ten pounds for all the ten lots and would give them to the church, challenging anyone to bid against him. They were immediately knocked down to him to the cheers of the crowd, and the vicar and churchwardens later presented their Jewish benefactor with an address of thanks from the entire parish!

In September 1851 he became curate of the parish of St Bartholomew's, Salford, taking his first baptism there on the 7th. He probably left Miriam and Charles in the safe keeping of Charles and Sarah Ashton. In Salford, it seems that as ever he was much thought of, and acquired there many friends: the Mouncey family, J. Horrocks, R. Billington, H. Stowell, J.C. Isard, T. Barton, to mention a few. In February he preached a sermon in St Bartholemew's on the subject of the terrible disaster which had just befallen Holmfirth; he called it 'Holmfirth's Solemn Voice', and he arranged for the text to be published.

The Holmfirth tragedy must have reminded him poignantly of his days in Tunis when the *Avenger* came to grief. In the early morning of Thursday, 5th February, 1852, as a result of a torrential storm, the Bilberry Reservoir burst its banks and a deluge of water came thundering down the valley, flooding the Yorkshire town of Holmfirth. Eighty one lives were lost, and thousands of people from the surrounding villages rushed into the town centre at day-break to view the devastation. To quote from the *London Illustrated News* of 14th February: 'The streets were filled with broken furniture, carding machines, huge iron boilers, bags of wool and other things; and the graveyards had their dead dislodged, and their contents borne again to the doors of the living.' Poems and articles were written about the catastrophe, and Moses added his sermon to the literary output dedicated to the tragedy. In arranging for it to be printed and published, he donated the proceeds to the general funds collected. More than enough was raised, and the excess was used to build five almshouses on New Mill Road in the town.

The sermon itself (published by Wertheim and Macintosh, together with Simms and Dinham of St Ann's Square, Manchester) was dedicated to the Revd J. Moore, BA the incumbent of St Bartholomew's, and under whom he was serving as curate. 'Coming events cast their shadows before' was his theme. He quoted the 'eighteen upon whom the tower in Siloam fell,' the plagues suffered by the Egyptians and the sacking of Carthage – the latter remind-ing him of the desolation he could see from the window of his room in Tunis. Show mercy to the poor, repent of your sins, he told his congregation, and such calamities will not occur. It was a Victorian view, but he did also express great sympathy for those who had suffered from the tragedy.

It was during these years when he was at Tranmere and Salford that he took an intense interest in Freemasonry; he was inevitably fascinated by the allusions and mysteries of the Craft to which he had been introduced some years earlier. In 1850, while at Tranmere, he joined the Cestrian Lodge of Chester, and in the history of the Lodge he is described as 'a converted Jew and a great Masonic lecturer.' In the same year he was appointed chaplain of the lodge. On 16th September, 1851, by now at Salford, he was unanimously elected a joining member of the Lodge of Virtue, meeting at the Albion Hotel. On November 18th he proposed the Revd Patrick Charles Nicholson, and on 27th December, William Greenwood, to be joining members of the lodge, and on this latter date here too he was invested as its chaplain. On 17th February, 1852, and again on 20th April, he delivered lectures at the lodge meetings. With his first-hand knowledge of Palestine he was able to speak with authority about Jerusalem – that 'point within a circle' – and he alludes to the Holy City and King Solomon's temple and their relevance to Freemasonry, giving also an account of some of his adventures and discoveries made in the course of his pilgrimage.

The Masonic lectures which he gave at this time, confirmed his reputation. He visited not only in the Manchester area, but also went as far afield as Nantwich, speaking at the King's Friends Lodge, whose warrant had been issued as early as 1793. One of his Manchester lectures, delivered in the Lodge of Virtue, was entitled, 'Vestiges of Genuine Freemasonry among the Ruins of Asia, Africa, etc.' in which he proudly displayed the knowledge and expertise he had gained during his travels in 1847–8. He dedicated the lecture to one Wolley Foster Esq., Senior Warden of the 'Worthy and Worshipful Lodge of Virtue'. He described his friend Foster as a 'worthy and exemplary' member of the St Bartholomew's congregation, and in doing so he invoked a 'blessing from the Great Architect of the Universe on all his undertakings'. His praise of this gentleman was fulsome; he was, he said, 'a fine example of husband, father and both public and private individual.' On this same occasion he went on to mention the recent lodge meeting when the Bible on which George

Washington had been obligated was ceremoniously paraded before the brethren.[1] This interesting relic, one of the spoils of war, belonged to the officers of the Lodge of Her Majesty's 46th Regiment of Infantry then stationed at Salford barracks. One of their number, a Captain Child, had the responsibility of its safe keeping. It had come into their possession during the course of military operations in the United States, and for a number of years had been carefully preserved by them when the regiment had been stationed in Halifax, Novia Scotia. Also during the course of this lecture he proudly exhibited the valuable 'congregational amulet' which he had bought 'for a large sum' from a Rabbi in Nablous back in 1848. He also considered it appropriate to quote to them an extract from the Freemason's Quarterly Review of July, 1834: 'Should the sceptic still ask the utility of our order, let him ask of the hundreds of innocent children whom Masonic charity has clothed and whom Masonic virtue has trained in the paths of respectability and truth.'

On 7th January, 1852 he was elected a member of the Lodge of Harmony, Todmorden, having in turn been proposed by William Greenwood.[2] On 3rd March and again on 5th May, Moses delivered his lectures at Todmorden, and he was rewarded with a vote of thanks which was 'carried unanimously'. The lodge minutes record also that 'Brother Margoliouth replied in very clear and appropriate terms.' On 23rd February 1853, his friend William

[1] George Washington was a celebrated Freemason. The magnificent George Washington Masonic National Memorial is in Alexandria, Virginia, USA.
[2] William Greenwood was presumably from the Todmorden area and perhaps living and working in Manchester, his reason for joining the Lodge of Virtue. Greenwood is very much a West Yorkshire name; he could well have been a parishioner of St Bartholomew's, Salford, at that time.

Greenwood became Master of the lodge, and at the same meeting Moses was invested as Senior Warden, but after this date all references to him in the lodge minutes cease. He was shortly to move from the Manchester area, and living in south Cheshire would have made visits back to Chester, Manchester and Todmorden impracticable. These three lodges still exist, and each holds a position of antiquity and distinction in the world of Freemasonry. For a time Moses' interest had been almost an obsession, and it is sad that he found it had become impossible to maintain these connections which had no doubt brought him much pleasure. Nevertheless, his lectures remain a curious and lasting testimony to this transitory facet of his life.

On 4th January, 1853, Moses was proudly able to take the part of the father of the bride: his daughter Miriam was married to William Parker in the lovely old parish church of St Andrew, Bebington, on the Wirral (St Catherine's, Tranmere, was understandably avoided). The marriage certificate shows that William was the son of John Parker, farmer, and three witnesses who signed were members of the Ashton family of Tranmere – Eliza, Mary Louisa and Thomas Ashton, three of the Ashton children, and friends of Miriam during her schooldays. Moses was present, and the service was taken by his friend the Revd Patrick Nicholson; it is likely that she was married from Tranmere Lodge. There is no indication that Chaja attended.

*

In May, 1853, he preached his farewell sermon at St Bartholomew's. Leaving there was a poignant moment for him. He had enjoyed the parish and had made many friends, but he felt it was time to move on once more. He gave his sermon the title: 'The Apostolic Triple Benediction', taking as his text 2 Corinthians 13:14: the

Grace. He considered his departure a solemn and important moment, and without ado he first dealt head-on with criticism from some quarters regarding his tendency to be personal in his sermons. This was a totally unjust complaint, he said. 'If I happened to allude to inconsistencies on the part of many professing Christians, the allusion was made generally and not particularly.' At the same time he maintained that it was proper, and indeed part of his duty, to remonstrate with a guilty conscience. In just the same way, he argued, St Paul had written to the Church at Corinth. 'I have reason to be thankful,' he said, 'on my taking leave of you, that according to my humble powers or insignificant abilities, I have not swerved from declaring unto you all the Counsel of God.' To those who desisted he said, 'I once more beseech you who are without Christ, bethink yourselves of your perilous condition.'

He expressed gratitude for the opportunities he had enjoyed of communion with the Sunday School teachers – this was obviously a vital part of the church life in the parish. His weekly meetings always left him 'invigorated', and he hoped this work would continue. In giving them the final triple benediction, he told them of his next move – 'I am about to enter upon a new and very extensive sphere of labour amongst strangers.' Finally, and with much emotion, he quoted;

> Christian brethren, 'ere we part,
> Ev'ry voice, and ev'ry heart,
> One glad hymn to God should raise,
> One high song of grateful praise.

Here we all may meet no more,
But there is a happier shore;
There released from toil and pain,
Brethren we shall meet again.

Now to God, the three in one,
Be eternal, Glory done;
Raise, ye saints, the strain again,
Gladly sound the loud Amen.

There can hardly have been a dry eye in the congregation.

★

He moved directly to Wybunbury, south Cheshire, to serve under the Revd James Hayes. To quote from diocesan records: '21st May. Commission to the Venerable Isaac Wood, clerk, Archdeacon of Chester and the Reverend Andrew Fuller Chater, clerk, Rector of Nantwich in the County of Chester, to qualify the Reverend Moses Margoliouth, clerk, to the stipendiary curacy of Wybunbury in the said County of Chester'. And then on 2nd June: 'Licence of the Reverend Moses Margoliouth, clerk, to the stipendiary curacy of the Reverend James Hayes, clerk, Vicar of the same church. Stipend £100.' On 19th May he had already started work, taking the wedding of James Sproson of Shavington, butcher, and Elizabeth Coomer.

St Chad's, Wybunbury, was one of the largest parishes in the country – 'an extensive sphere' – but in 1853 congregations there were small, as he had been advised in a letter from James Hayes dated the 19th April: 'The congregation has now dwindled to a very small one, but I trust your message will soon call back the wanderers and many others.' This was a word of warning, and Moses wrote shortly afterwards: 'Notwithstanding the preparation, my heart sunk (sic) within me when I looked round the church on my first Sunday amongst you. Few and far between was the attendance, which made the spacious church look empty.' He soon came to realise that the cause of the problem was the health of the vicar; during Moses' time at Wybunbury, James Hayes did not preach a single sermon, and 'very very seldom read prayers on a Sunday afternoon.'

Moses at once set about his parochial duties, and was helped in his work by the Revd Delves Broughton of Broughton Hall, Staffordshire, vicar of the adjoining small parish of Doddington. The Revd James Folliott of Stapeley House, a well-to-do clergyman residing in the parish, also assisted when the need arose in the matter of weddings and funerals.

It was during Lent, 1854, that Moses was given the task of preaching a series of sermons – nine in all – in the Parish Church, each dealing with aspects of the Book of the Prophet Hosea. The main theme on which he dwells in these sermons is the need for repentance. God has an unchangeable love towards his people, and yet they (in this case Israel), are sinking deeper and deeper into the mire of sin. On the other hand, 'no sooner are the Children of Israel brought to a sense of their helpless wretchedness... and led to ask for pardon and mercy, than they obtain grace.' The Lord pours the balm of consolation into their wounded spirits. It is interesting that he discusses at length the Prodigal Son, who left home to visit a far-off land; he is like Israel and has, provided that the repentance is genuine, the same chance of salvation. In the fourth sermon he refers to the impending war with Turkey: 'Brethren, we are now alarmed at the probable interruption of worldly peace, by reason of the fearful war, which is at present threatening the civilised world. And well we might, for it is a war likely to prove unprecedented in the annals of martial enterprize (sic).' His travels in 1847–8 naturally made him feel close to the scene of the impending conflict, unlike his congregation to whom it must have appeared remote. Peace was of course desirable, he argued, but international peace could not possibly compare with the soul's peace with God. The latter sort of peace could only be achieved by penitence; provided this is sincere, God will promise, and eventually grant, forgiveness, and the New Jerusalem would be created with all the grandeur and perfection of the original Temple of King Solomon. He refers in this context to the beauty of the olive tree, and he points out that the wood from this tree was honoured by the place it occupied in the Temple. At the same time, Moses casts his mind back to his time in the Holy Land: 'Many a morning, whilst riding on Mount Lebanon, did I taste the peculiar deliciousness of its balmy air; and a sweet perfume emanated from its dust when first disturbed by the hoofs of my horse.' His ninth sermon overran the Lenten period, and was actually delivered on the morning of the second Sunday after Easter. He finished with a warning, 'With whom do you wish to be classed? With the just or with the transgressors? With the just, He may give you grace and strength to walk in His ways; if not, then I have not shunned from warning you of the consequences.'

At this time, he was alone, away from his family, and in a fresh environment. Parts of the parish were, to quote his own description, 'very ignorant' and he was for the first time working in a genuinely remote and rural parish. Although in a situation of his own making, he must often have had feelings of loneliness and regret; these sentiments were unquestionably reflected in the Wybunbury sermons, and there is a sad poignancy in his comments on the unfortunate Hosea. There is no doubt that the 'very important' chapter fourteen disguised inner feelings which were totally hidden from his congregation.

A further matter soon began to cause him concern and

anxiety. James Hayes, the devoted servant of Wybunbury for so long, had become really ill, both physically and mentally, and any parochial work had become quite beyond his powers. This slowly led to an episode in Moses' career which was something of an ecclesiastical *cause célèbre* – a tortuous affair, which gives remarkable insight into the jealousies and tensions which can obtrude into church life, perhaps associated more with the cathedral close of Trollope than a real live country parish in Cheshire. In fact, as 1854 wore on, almost the full burden of the parish rested on Moses' shoulders. It was certainly true that under his charge, church attendance increased from 'a few tens, to as many hundreds'. Moses was 'largely instrumental in the speedy erection of a new school', (in the Broad Lane township), 'in a most neglected and destitute part of the parish'. After several months of difficulty which had been the result of James Hayes' failing abilities, once again 'the poor and sick were visited and had the Gospel preached to them'. The problem that now arose was the result of a legal nicety relating to the Pastoral Aid Society, whose grant was largely responsible for the payment of the wages of Wybunbury's curate. It was an odd rule of the Society that it could not supply funds to parishes where the incumbent was incapable of performing the parochial duties himself. This seems strange in that one would imagine it was in such a situation that the grant would naturally become even more vital, but it was intended that a curate should be assisting an *active* incumbent; to be supplying funds for the entire running of a parish was not the purpose of the Pastoral Aid Society. Indeed at regular intervals parishes were checked by means of a questionnaire, and if things failed to conform to the rules, the grant was withdrawn forthwith. In fact, as Moses wrote in January, 1855, 'the aid would have been discontinued last year, were it not for my undertaking a third service on the Lord's Day'. It was even said at the time that the vicar was guilty of an act of gross fraud towards the society by accepting the grant under the existing circumstances! The situation was absurd, and the parish was in turmoil. The sad fact was that Moses had no alternative but to look for a position elsewhere. It was for this reason that a number of parishioners, including the two wardens (George Pigott and Robert Adams) sent a memorial to the Bishop requesting that their curate should somehow be enabled to remain. This plea was sent to Chester on 22nd January, 1855:

> We, the undersigned, members of this parish, situated in your Lordship's diocese, take the liberty of appealing to you in our present emergency and spiritual exigency. We have reason to apprehend that we are about to be left again without a spiritual guide or instructor. For nearly two years have we been favoured with the ministrations of the Revd M. Margoliouth, and during that period he has devoted all his time, energy, and strength to the spiritual requirements of this vast and extensive district. He has alone performed three full services on the Sabbath day, and attended personally to the Sunday schools morning and afternoon. He has held three weekly lectures, in distant parts and dark corners of the parish, and was instrumental in the speedy erection of a new school. Ever since the Revd M. Margoliouth came amongst us, he has laboured single-handed; as the vicar, in consequence of bodily and mental infirmity, can do nothing. Our Curate's work, we are thankful to say, has been crowned with success in a variety of ways.
>
> But we are threatened because it is contrary to the rules of the Pastoral Aid Society to grant a Curate to a parish whose Incumbent is incapable of performing

the duty – to be deprived of the services of our highly-esteemed Curate. Your Lordship, therefore, will kindly bear with our earnest importunities, when we express our urgent solicitude, to interpose your influence and authority, in order to provide for us permanent and uninterrupted watchfulness, by securing for us the efficient services of our present able minister.

Beneath this are many signatures, (sixty-three), with the note: 'Your Lordship will be pleased kindly to bear in mind, that many more signatures would have been added, had time and weather permitted.'

The complex plot slowly became more sinister: the secretary of the committee of the Pastoral Aid Society had written to James Hayes giving details of the Tranmere Affair and Moses' dispute with Mr Arthure. It seems that the Society, and no doubt others, were determined to get rid of him, and Moses had now become the victim of slurs and innuendo which finally had come to cloud his relationship with James Hayes. As at Tranmere, Moses' success in Wybunbury parish had worked against him and had activated jealousy and venom. The fact is that the pleas of the parishioners received no response in Chester, and the little Jew was being sent on his way.

He did not go quietly. The patient shrug was not his style. On his last Sunday, he preached a sermon to his parishioners (for such he felt he had a right to call them), stating his case, and expressing his farewells. Many people had stood by him, but not all. He detailed the full facts of the case, and told them of the support he had received from Tranmere – not least from his loyal friend Charles Ashton. Both the Chancellor and the Bishop had spoken of his sincerity. 'All these particulars were well known to the principal inhabitants of this parish,' he told them, 'yet a certain individual, whose position ought to have taught him to regard – but alas! his disposition leads him to disregard – *truth and justice*, had the assurance to repeat on Wednesday 31st January, the falsehood, (in a place where brotherly love and truth are essential principles), that I was the cause of the loss of the Pastoral Aid Society's grant to Wybunbury.' He went on to explain that this 'individual' had done his best to persuade the Bishop on the subject. Almost certainly he was pointing his finger at the Revd James Folliott of Stapeley House. He was in a position to know the Bishop. He was a prominent Freemason (as Moses was implying), and his name was conspicuously absent from the memorial to the Bishop. Crucially and sadly his vicar, who had hitherto remained loyal to his industrious assistant, turned against him. On 3rd January he had the following letter from Mr Hayes' attorney:

Reverend Sir, Mr Hayes, as you are aware, is far from well, and very unequal to any business which may distress his feelings and has therefore deputised me to communicate to you, that he has, after mature consideration and a conference with others, decided to terminate his engagement with you, as his curate, and which you will therefore consider at an end from the beginning of February next, which, I understand, completes the year.

I am, Revd Sir, Your faithful servant,

E.D. Broughton[3]

It is hard to imagine his feelings during those last few weeks in Wybunbury. But he had often shown heroism in the past, and it was not in his nature to dwell on the shadows,

---

[3] Edward Delves Broughton – a kinsman of Revd D. Broughton (see above).

even though shadows certainly existed, and maybe there was an element of escape as he moved from place to place; perhaps it was a way of dispelling the gloom. At the same time, as he had implied in the dedication prefixed to the sermons, it had never been his intention to stay in that part of the Lord's 'worldwide vineyard' for long. Early in February 1855, he took his last service at Wybunbury (a wedding between John Hulse and Sarah Dobson), once again said his goodbyes, and set out east for Lincolnshire.

★

There, conveniently close to the east coast port of Hull, which had given him his first sight of England, Moses now came to live, and serve as curate for some months in the small and attractive village of Great Coates, near Grimsby. Its fine old church is dedicated to St Nicholas. A little later, in the 1870s, local society was rife with talk of the famous 'Great Coates Case'. The local squire, Sir Richard Sutton, sold his life interest in the Great Coates advowson to a clergyman who presented himself at the living on the death of the Revd Henry Houson. The Bishop of Lincoln, then Dr Christopher Wordsworth, refused to institute the newcomer on the grounds that the 'cure of souls' should not be bought or sold. The case was taken to the Court of Common Pleas. The Bishop won his case, but it dragged on until 1875 when the Revd Wm Walsh was instituted by the Archbishop of Canterbury by virtue of a special writ from the Queen. When the time came, Moses no doubt followed this affair with special interest.

With bitter memories of both Tranmere and Wybunbury, he was soon to set sail and return, for a time, to the land of his birth. He would also visit Russia, Turkey, Italy and Germany, in which countries he would be able to practice his linguistic skills, and for an interlude of some

122

eighteen months he would enjoy fresh sights and sounds, and recall memories of his youth. His father had died, almost certainly in 1852,[4] but he would, with a degree of apprehension, see again his family, in particular his dear mother, to whom, in the pursuit of his vision, he had brought great pride, tinged with anguish and disappointment.

[4] Jewish grandchildren were never given the name of their grandfather in his lifetime, and George (Gershon), son of Moses' brother Herschel, was born in 1853. See also Appendix V.

Chapter VII
To Moscow and Back

The eighteen months he was away from England in 1856–7 were the outcome of a well laid and ambitious plan, and there is no doubt that he had placed himself near to Hull as a convenient point of departure. At the time he left England, Chaja was living in Paris, Miriam was safely married and Charles was in the care of the Ashtons. There are no letters extant to detail his travels across Europe as was the case with his adventures on his pilgrimage, but he went first to Suwalki (almost certainly back via Hamburg), and for a time he was reunited with his widowed mother and the rest of the family remaining in his home town. It must have been an exciting time for all of them, and he was no doubt welcomed back like the prodigal son. The extent and duration of his travels covering this period are sufficient proof that kindness was showered upon him, and he must have received from his mother sufficient means to cover his journeys, both travel and accommodation.

From Suwalki he eventually set out for Moscow. En route he visited his brother Herschel and family then living in Vilkaviskis, some fifty miles directly north, on the main road west from Kapsukas toward Konigsberg. He made an impression on his small nephew Gershon, named after the boy's grandfather – very much a Jewish tradition; sons rarely bear their father's name. Young George Margoliouth appears later in this story. He too was destined to become a convert to Christianity, and later in the century was

124

ordained in England.

Moses was in Moscow in September 1856, at the time of the enthronement, in the Kremlin, of Alexander II. The elaborate celebrations organised by the Court included a small orchestra which played the Russian national anthem in a submarine in Kronstadt Harbour, St Petersberg. True to form, Moses entered into the proceedings by preaching a 'Coronation Sermon' in the English Chapel[1] on the Sunday before the coronation, which took place on 7th September.

He entitled his address, 'The Lord's Anointed', and dedicated it to the Revd William Gray, BA, minister of the chapel. While staying in Moscow he was generously given hospitality by Mr Gray, at whose request, as he succinctly recorded at the time, 'I accordingly prepared what I thought a suitable sermon, and I preached it.' He declared at the time that he had become interested in the state and condition of the chapel there, along with its associated schools. In his opinion Mr Gray lacked support, and he later, with his usual enthusiasm, had the sermon printed in London, and directed the proceeds of sale to go towards bringing the Moscow parish to the attention of the public.

He suitably took as his text 2 Kings 11:12: 'And he brought forth the king's son, and put the crown upon him, and gave him the testimony; and they made him king, and anointed him; and they clapped their hands and said, God save the King.' It was a wonderful chance for him to express his long held, almost fanatical, admiration for the system of monarchy and its spiritual association, which he had poetically demonstrated in his Hebrew poem of 1842. It was vital, he said, that a new reign was given a 'baptism,' along with the Church's blessing. The new Tzar, no matter how wise and powerful, needed the anointment of his enthronement, which was about to take place in the

---

[1] Now St Andrew's Anglican Church in Moscow.

Kremlin. We have monarchs, he told the congregation, to 'pre-figure the coming of Him whom St John describes – and I saw Heaven opened and behold a white horse. His eyes were as a flame of fire, and on His head were many crowns.' This was heady material for his listeners, mostly English, and he assured them that they had good reason to join with the Russian people in both joys and petitions on behalf of his Imperial Majesty. With great diplomacy he said that apart from a few interruptions the relationship between Russia and Great Britain had been close. 'It is indeed our duty,' he continued, 'to look on Alexander as the *Lord's Anointed*'.

From Moscow he made his way to Odessa, the Crimea and then down to Constantinople, the scene of his memorable visit eight years earlier. Little is known of his return journey, but, on leaving Constantinople, he sailed down the Aegean of which he quaintly recounted the following episode of near-mutiny:

'The ship I sailed in was an Italian one, commanded by a captain of the same nation. The captain could not perceive, in the dusk of the evening, an island at which we were going with perilous speed. I saw the island, and pointed it out to my fellow passengers and the captain. The latter was obstinate and would not see, and the former became panic-stricken and began to nibble at the small boats. 'What!' I exclaimed, 'and leave the rest of the passengers and crew to perish with the ship?'

'But what is to be done when the besotted captain will not see the danger?'

'Let us bind him hand and foot, and change our course; the mates and sailors are with us: some of us know sufficient of navigation to avert the impending catastrophe.' The advice was acted upon, and all were saved, the ship and captain included.'

At some stage he was in Rome where he spent time in

museums and libraries there, perhaps sailing from Turkey to the west coast of Italy. He then made his way north to Nuremburg, where he studied for some months at the University of Erlangen – surely confirming the comment he made in 1843: 'My dear father... never considered any expense too extravagant where learning could be got.' The University there was founded in the eighteenth century, originally in Bayreuth, and in 1743 was transferred to Erlangen. It is situated a little to the north of Nuremberg, almost at the point where the rivers Schwabach and Regnitz meet. The palace there was formerly the seat of the Margraves of Kulmbach-Bayreuth, and it now forms the main building of the University.

In the Spring of 1857 he was presented with a PhD degree from the university. This was to some extent honorary, although he did study there, under Professor Dr Karl Friedrich Nagelsbach (1806–1859), who had been Professor of Philology at Erlangen since 1842. The award of the degree was actually confirmed on 30th April, by which time he was back in England. The university acknowledged his writings and expertise in the Hebrew language. To quote from their archives: 'OB EGREGIAM EBRAICARUM LITERATUM ET HAUD VULGAREM HISTORIARUM IMPRIMIS JUDAICAE GENTIS SCIENTIAM LIBRIS COMPLURIBUS EDITIS ABUNDE COMPROBATAM'.

It is likely that he visited Berlin during his travels, but it is certain that soon after leaving Nuremberg, early in 1857, Moses returned to England and became curate in the small prosperous town of Braintree in Essex. His latest 'pilgrimage' had brought complete restitution and understanding with his family, and both they and he could be proud of the recognition of his academic and literary achievements which had been generously bestowed upon him at Erlangen. Now he was again, and in yet another part of the Lord's Vineyard, to resume the work of a parish curate, exercising his talents in a new environment. His short time in Braintree seems to have been a lively one and, as usual, he made a number of friends on whom he could rely and, as in Dublin, he found himself in a coterie well able to offer him an intellectual rapport which suited him.

He took three funerals in Braintree Parish Church in March, in each case signing himself as 'officiating minister', suggesting that his formal appointment had not yet been made, but his signature as curate started on 3rd April 1857, and he was taking services there up to the 25th June, 1858. His address during his time there was 'Prospect House'.

On 7th October, 1857, he delivered a sermon in Braintree entitled 'The Quarrel of God's Covenant: a fast-day sermon'. As with the Wybunbury sermons, he arranged for it to be printed locally, in this case by Joscelyne and Son of Braintree, and published in London by Wertheim and Macintosh.

It became something of a *cause célèbre*. It was certainly an example of the fearless stand he was prepared to take on matters of principle and controversy. There had recently been fierce opposition in the town to the church rate levied, and demonstrators had disrupted services. 'This parish,' Moses proclaimed from the pulpit, 'is an awful illustration of the irreverence shown to the sanctuary of God.' It was just and proper, he argued, that a tax should be exacted from the people to contribute towards the religion of their country. The rate was based on property, as it had been from time immemorial. He then went further in his condemnation of the citizens of Braintree: 'For instance on the Sunday when we commemorated the dying love of our Lord Jesus... scarcely one tenth of the congregation drew near to the table of the Lord.' His outrage was uncompro-mising: 'How are the young and ignorant cared for? I might again adduce the state of this parish as a melancholy illustration.' Divine judgement was threatening them all, and he quoted such events as the Armada and the fate of Napoleon. 'Jehovah,' he warned them, 'is the God of Battles.' He extended his argument to the nation as a whole: wars are ceaseless and are punishment for sins committed. The war with Russia had only recently ended, followed by a war with China. In his words: 'Our nation is endeavouring to chastise the arrogant miscreant of Canton.' He went on: 'We have no hesitation in saying that we consider the fatal and dire mutiny in India as a voice from heaven.' And he told them that there was no escape from these international upheavals – 'The facilities of locomotion and that wonderful agency the electric telegraph render every occurrence trumpet-tongued throughout the length and breadth of this mighty kingdom.' Then back to his old theme 'Except ye repent, ye shall all likewise perish!'

Braintree was stunned. But he had spoken his mind and many, maybe most, respected him for his straight talk. In fact he acquired many friends in the district. One example was the distinguished Round family. John Round had been High Steward of Colchester in 1848; and Charles Gray Round of Birch Hall, Braintree, was Recorder of Colchester. Such men were clearly on his side when it came to church rates. He came to know Augustus Charles Veley, solicitor, of Great Square, later to be appointed Registrar of the Ecclesiastical Courts in the diocese. Miss Fanny Wakeham was a devotee – she lived in London Road – and Edward George Craig, another solicitor, of Mount House in the town was in his circle of friends, and he also struck up an acquaintance with a neighbouring clergyman, the Revd J.C. Ryle, rector of Helmingham. Another lawyer he came to know was Augustus Cunnington, Registrar of the County Court. Moses was clearly popular with some, if not all, of the parishioners of Braintree, and with his usual facility he entered into the professional society of the town. But he grew restive, and soon felt the moment had come to give more time to his writing, including his grand project, the Hebrew Old Testament. Some time in July he left Braintree in order to give these matters more of his attention.

Chapter VIII
Emigration

It was in the following year, 1859, that a momentous event took place in the Margoliouth family which was to put a new twist into the course of its future. For a brief and shadowy appearance in this chapter, both of Moses' surviving children emerge from their dark corridor, and are seen as characters in their own right, determining for themselves the passages of their lives and those of their descendants. It no doubt caused Moses much anguish at the time, but had little effect on his own personal life and career.

Miriam and William, with their two children, Minnie (b. 1855) and William (b. 1857), decided to emigrate to New Zealand, and off they set in the sailing ship *Red Jacket*, (under Capt. Reed) arriving in Napier, Hawke's Bay, on the North Island. (Following their example, Charles joined them some years later – see below). Miriam, not for the first time in her life, was facing her future in a new country, this time on the other side of the world. With William and Miriam went William's brother Henry, and shortly after their arrival the two brothers went into partnership with one William Rich, as stockdealers, shippers and butchers and they employed a number of hands. In 1861, Miriam gave birth to her third child, Frederick.

In 1864, three of the Poverty Bay (north of Hawke's Bay) Maoris decided that too much of their land was lying idle, so they came south to Napier to see if they could find

Europeans to take up occupation. They met up with William and Henry, who, after due negotiation, took over twenty thousand acres on a twenty-one year lease, at a rental of two thousand pounds per annum with the right of first refusal to purchase.

The terrain was rough, in parts marshy, and covered with shrub and fern. To make a start, Henry took sheep to the property by ship, but he soon fell out with the Maoris when he put down poison to kill the Maoris' dogs which had been attacking his livestock. Henry became the recipient of severe threats, and in the end felt forced to return to Napier; he never went back to the property.

In 1866 Robert Thelwall, a cousin of the Parkers, joined them from England. He had recently inherited one thousand pounds – a small fortune – which enabled him to purchase land in the area of Poverty Bay alongside the Parker property, and with this added incentive, Miriam, with husband and family, along with Thelwall, set sail from Napier in the *Cleopatra*, a small paddle steamer, to live and establish themselves on their land in Poverty Bay – in what is now the town of Gisborne.[1] Instead of building a homestead for themselves, they took the lease of a large house on the south side of the river Taruheru. The building was substantial, and had formerly been the home of the resident magistrate for the area, H.S. Wardell. It was situated near to what are now called the Roseland Gardens, and close to where the Roseland Hotel was later to be built. The house was on the opposite side of the river to the Parker land, and in order to pass from one to the other, they used a rope stretched over the water to enable them, seated in a canoe, to pass backwards and forwards. About thirty people then lived in what was later to become Gisborne, so their

---

[1] Very near to the historic spot where Captain Cook first landed in New Zealand, October, 1769.

William Parker.

Mrs William Parker.
(Moses' daughter Miriam.)

Maria Theresa,
Charles Margoliouth's wife.

William Parker junior.

Moses' granddaughter,
Minnie Parker.

community was small and vulnerable. On the other hand it was a peaceful, if labour-intensive and primitive, lifestyle. Miriam, along with other settlers' wives, cooked in a camp oven and water had to be fetched from a source some distance away; old clothes had to be sewn and patched; mending and making do was the order of the day.

On Sunday, 9th November, 1868, all was peaceful, although Miriam had had premonitions of trouble. Her breeding and the experiences of her early years were about to stand her in good stead. The Maoris were dissatisfied; they felt great resentment towards the white settlers, and had murder on their minds. The Parker household that night consisted of Miriam and William, two sons William and Frederick, Robert Thelwall, C. Smale, Daniel Munns and Bob Parkhouse. Minnie and baby John, born earlier that year, were by chance staying with friends nearby. There was tension in the air. Between three and four in the morning (it was now Monday), a rifle shot was heard, and Messrs Smale, Munns, Parkhouse and Thelwall, who were members of the Poverty Bay Mounted Rifles, armed themselves to the teeth and went out to face the enemy. They were all about to endure what became known as the Poverty Bay Massacre.

The Parkers escaped by the skin of their teeth. Miriam, William and their children, clad only in their night attire, ran out into the cover of the trees near the house. Munns, mounted on his horse, raced off to warn other settlers. Smale and co. fled with their guns into the surrounding countryside as best they could. A number of settlers were killed, but Miriam and William and their entire family managed to escape with their lives. The two other Parker children, staying with friends, made for the shore and also managed to reach safety. Minnie, only a little girl of thirteen, not only carried her baby brother for the greater part of their flight, but also had had the presence of mind to fill his bottle before she left. (Later the citizens of Napier subscribed towards a suitable gift for the brave child).

In spite of this trauma[2] – an experience which was to be recalled with horror throughout the rest of their lives – the Parkers stayed on for some years, but as time went by William found it more and more difficult to control and develop the land, and they eventually gave up and returned to Napier, where William found other employment.

Moses' son Charles also emigrated to New Zealand, probably in the mid 1860s, no doubt at the suggestion and recommendation of his sister. He had failed to find profitable employment in England, and decided that he too would seek his fortune on the other side of the world. He there met and married a young widow, Maria Theresa Carter, who had three daughters[3] and by her Charles became the father of four children: Vera, Charles Ernest Lindsay, Iolanthe and Lionel. Thus, in due course, he had the responsibility of seven children in all.

Charles' wife was the granddaughter of William and Douglas Mary McKain, who for a time lived in Cheadle, Staffordshire. In 1837 William was killed in a hunting accident, and the self-reliant and determined widow then, in 1841, decided to emigrate, with her four surviving sons and youngest daughter, Robina, to New Zealand, leaving behind, much to her distress, four married daughters. They sailed on the *Olympus*, and as emigration is the subject of this chapter, it is interesting to quote two letters this valiant lady wrote to her daughters back home, the first during the course of the voyage; it gives something of the atmosphere of such an adventurous trip, no doubt similar to those undertaken by Miriam and Charles just a few years later:

---

[2] European settlement was held back in this part of New Zealand due to this and other similar incidents at this period.

[3] Her daughter Ethel was the grandmother of Gerald Hansard, referred to elsewhere – see Acknowledgements, and Preface.

My beloved children,

As there is a ship in sight I take the opportunity of writing a few lines to let you know we are all in good health and spirits. I wrote to you and to Mary, to Mrs Waugh, and to Nathan Loton on 10th Jan. by the ship *Whitby*, of London, bound for Cork. We passed five vessels that day. The captain went on board the Whitby with six of the cabin passengers and then the Whitby came actually alongside of the Olympus to the great terror of most of us who could see the danger of two such ponderous machines coming so near each other. To add to the terror of the two commanders, the vessels refused to answer the helms and I fully expected the next move would crush them together. The seamen had to cut some of our ropes, and then to our great joy the space between the vessels widened. The Whitby dropped astern and soon after our captain and the other gentlemen came on board and brought a Cape sheep with them. The *Whitby* soon after left us and we gave them three cheers which her crew returned.

We spoke to only one of the other vessels, the Jane of Glasgow, [also] bound for New Zealand. She came near us at 6 o'clock in the evening, and our captain invited her captain to breakfast with him next morning, which invitation was accepted, and the Jane lay to for us all night. But we kept her at a respectful distance as we had been dreadfully alarmed by the too near approach of the *Whitby*.

Next morning brought the captain and three gentlemen of the Jane, bringing to our captain a present of fruit which they had brought from St Jagos where they had remained two or three days. I got one of the bananas which is a most delicious fruit. They stopped on board about two hours, and then left us. They saluted us with one of their cannons, which our people returned by a discharge of small arms. She was soon out of sight as she was a much faster sailer than the Olympus.

On 15th Jan. we crossed the Line at 9 o'clock in the morning. Our superintendent, Dr Featherston, ordered a glass of rum to be served out to each adult. In the evening the sailors claimed the privilege of introducing Neptune and his wife on board. But there was no shaving or any ribaldry to extort money. Everyone who chose to give did it freely. I gave them 1/-, as much as I could afford. The sailors collected about £3 and they finished the evening's amusement with a song.

Your brothers and sister are well and happy. James works very hard helping the second mate getting the emigrants' stores out of the hold. If you were to see him sometimes you would think he was just come out of the coal pit.

I wrote you an account of the storm we encountered in the Bay of Biscay, but the danger from the Whitby's proximity to us on the 10th was more apparent and the captain was more alarmed.

We have plenty of good provisions. The water is getting very bad but we have it mixed for drinking with lime juice and sugar one day and next day half a pint of grog.

On 27th Jan. there was a fine boy born on board and he and the mother are doing well. On 29th we got out of the tropics so the most unhealthy part of our voyage is over. There have been three deaths on board, all children, which I think is not many in so long and perilous a voyage.

One of the emigrants has a violin and plays on it

most evenings and many of the people dance on deck. We have singing and jokes of all sorts, and as a contrast, a man was put in irons one day for striking his wife. The assistant superintendent is not liked and has, this week, been suspended for striking one of the emigrants. So you see we have sport of all sorts.

Robina is teaching a class of children.

Kiss my dear children for me and tell them that one day the sea all around the ship was covered with great fish called porpoises. There seemed to be thousands of them. We have also seen a great number of what the sailors call black fish which are very large.

I have got into the way of making nice light bread. The steward gave me a small piece of yeast and showed me how to mix it and from time to time I save a piece and by that means have a constant supply of fresh bread. If we had double the quantity of flour and half the quantity of biscuits we should do well. Each adult has 2 lbs of flour a week, but I soak a little biscuit in water to a pulp and mix it with my flour either for bread or pudding. But I did not bring spices or carbonate of soda with me which was a great neglect. Oh! we do so long for a little cheese. The little we brought with us was much appreciated while it lasted.

There is some misunderstanding between the superintendent and the captain. They do not associate, nor do they dine at the same table. Our potatoes are all used and we have rice instead. Our tea is served out dry, and our coffee raw, and we roast it ourselves, which we much prefer to do.

Captain White says if this wind continues we shall be in New Zealand in another month.

The boys have lost five caps since we came on board. One of the cabin passengers lost two hats overboard in one day. I have lost several towels when drying them, a new flannel waistcoat of John's and an apron of Robina's. By-the-by she is a great favourite on board. John often wishes you were all with us. So do I if you could have come safely. I think Robina was never so happy in all her life.

April 20th, 1841. Here we are at last. We anchored about 10.30 this morning, but will not get on shore this day. A vessel sails for London tomorrow so I embrace the opportunity of sending this by her. I will write to you by the next opportunity.

God bless you, my dear children. Kiss your dear little boys for me. We are all well and in high spirits. The vessel I send this by is called the Lord Brougham. Write to me every month. The place looks very mountainous, but the people who came on board give a good account of it. We have had an excellent doctor and captain.

Your affectionate Mother,

D.M. McKain. Adieu, Adieu.

Mrs McKain's next letter to her daughters back in England gives an interesting glimpse into her early days in the colony:

My dear Children,

The Olympus entered Cook's Straits at 8 o'clock at night, 17th April and we cleared them on the 18th at 10 p.m. The approach to New Zealand is most unpromising. On the morning of the 19th, when I went on deck I saw no appearance of vegetation on the land, but a bold, barren rocky or clay coast on every side. All the emigrants were very low-spirited.

We anchored that night for the first time since we left the Downs. The next morning the anchor was weighed again and we soon entered Port Nicholson where a very different prospect met our view. The mountains are completely covered with timber, reaching within a quarter of a mile of the water's edge. Here are the most beautiful shrubs in full bloom, although I am told this is reckoned one of the worst months in the year, and it is indeed a season of storms.

We finally anchored on the 20th. On the 21st it began to blow hard, and towards night the gale increased to such a height that although we had both anchors out the vessel drifted dreadfully and we were every hour in expectation of being dashed on the rocks. But, thank God, the wind abated and we all came safely on shore on the 23rd, and as fine a day as any I ever knew in England in summer. The fine weather continued for a few days and then it began to blow and rain, and the rain came pouring down through the roofs of the Depot houses until everything was wet and miserable. And what makes it more wretched there are no fireplaces in the houses. We make fires out of doors to cook by.

On the morning of the 25th we were ordered to attend at the camp stores for our rations. John and James brought home 35 lbs of beef and pork, with tea and sugar for Robina and myself, and on the following week we had the same rations served out by the company's agent. Then we drew from the ship's stores that had been stopped over and above what we made use of on board – 31 lbs of rice, 34 lbs split peas, 5 lbs of raisins, 350 lbs of biscuits and a quantity of pickled cabbage, mustard and salt, with 131 lbs of salt beef.

I have taken a piece of land as level as your house floor. The lease cost £4, the rent £12 a year for seven years. John and James are busy building a cottage on it. It is a most delightful situation. We have a full view of the harbour.

On 20th May the Lord William Bentinck, one of the Company ships, entered the harbour just that day month after the *Olympus* and on that day I received letters from my dear, dear children. It was your birthday and wedding day, dear Douglas; and it was Cheadle May Fair Day. Oh, I wept bitterly when reading your affectionate letters. Oh, may Almighty God comfort you. My dear Mary, I shall never ask you to follow me.

This is the winter here, yet some days it is most delightful and the sun quite hot. Then again it blows till we think the cottage will go over.

Things are very dear here. Skim milk 8d per quart. They do not sell the new milk; they make butter from the cream which they sell at 5/- per lb. Salt butter is 2/3d. per lb, and 9d. the 2 lb loaf; Soap is 7d and soda 8d per lb.

The cabin passengers are very dissatisfied with their situation as their sections of land lay a great way from the town. Some of them are selling their land for a third of what they paid for it, and some are going off to Sydney.

Captain White and Dr Featherston have given us a most excellent character to Colonel Wakefield and other gentlemen. The captain came to see me at the Depot and when he saw me so uncomfortable he told me that I must go on board and stay as long as the ship was in harbour. But I did not accept his kind invitation as I could not make myself content away from the family.

I have now been nearly two months in the colony. This is Whit Sunday and it is very cold. I think of you every hour of the day, and when I think of my dear native land, in a moment I seem to be there, but ah, recollections at hand soon hurry me back. No, not to despair, but to sorrow and love.

Oh, how I picture in my mind Julia busy with her dear little family, Mary always busy, Douglas at her domestic concerns and poor Eliza, what of her? Then I see you get together in deep lamentation over your poor old mother, your sister Robina, and your four dear brothers. Your brothers never regret having come out here. Frederick and Isaac are delighted. John and James seem very happy, but Robina and myself sigh after England. At least, I sigh for the loved ones I left there. God bless you my dear ones. Pray for the exiles in New Zealand.
D.M. McKain.

In reading these poignant letters one cannot but admire the hope and trust of those brave nineteenth century settlers – of which, along with Mrs McKain and her family, Moses' two children were examples. So often facing hardship and disappointment, many of them must have found their enthusiasm difficult to sustain.[4] The woman who became Charles Margoliouth's wife, Maria, New Zealand born, was the daughter of James, one of the four confident McKain sons who had accompanied their resourceful mother. It was no doubt their zeal which had inspired the enterprise. Maria had previously been married to one Captain John

---

[4] It is perhaps comforting to know that two of Mrs McKain's daughters and their families eventually joined their mother in New Zealand. They were Julia and Mary. Julia's husband, Joseph Torr, became first member of the County Council for Petane in Hawke's Bay, and Mary's husband, John McCarthy, enjoyed a successful career in school and church building. Mrs McKain eventually went to live in the Esk Valley in Hawke's Bay. She died at Eskdale in 1873, aged 84.

Carter – John Chilton Lambton Carter 1816–1872. She had married him at the age of sixteen, as his second wife, the first Mrs Carter having died in 1861.[5] The Carters had arrived in New Zealand in 1852, and John took up six thousand acres of land in Hawke's Bay. In 1861 he became superintendent of the Hawke's Bay District, and in 1863 was made Captain of the Napier Regiment of Militia, in the same year becoming Commissioner of Crown Lands for Hawke's Bay. He died in 1872, and three years later his widow Maria married Charles Margoliouth, thus becoming Moses' daughter-in-law.[6]

It is probable that Charles and Maria and their family settled in the Gisborne area, even though the Parkers eventually returned to Napier. Descendants of Charles Ernest Lindsay Margoliouth (Charles' and Maria's elder son, and therefore Moses' grandson), still live in that part of New Zealand. The name Lindsay still persists in the

---

[5] The first Mrs Carter was Susan, daughter of Rear-Admiral James Lillicrap of Caroline Place, Stonehouse, Plymouth.

[6] It seems that during her widowhood Maria had received much help, advice and financial assistance from one Algernon Tollemache, who was then living nearby. He had been a friend of her late husband, and in fact had lent him money. Even after her marriage to Charles, Mr Tollemache continued to help and advise her after his return to England, where he lived in Richmond, Surrey. He was Algernon Gray Tollemache, M.P. for Grantham, 1832–37, b. 1805, d. 1892. It is interesting to note that Gerald Hansard of Gisborne, descended from Ethel, one of Charles Lindsay Margoliouth's step-daughters, remembers his father keeping documents in a metal deedbox labelled TOLLEMACHE. Algernon Tollemache married his cousin, Francis Louisa Tollemache. They had no children. One of Algernon's brothers was the Revd Hugh Francis Tollemache, whose grandson lived in New Zealand, perhaps having inherited land from Algernon, his grandfather's brother. This grandson's name was Lyulph Ydwallo Odin Nestor Egbert Lyonel Tiodmag Hugh Erchenwyne Saxon Esa Cromwell Orna Nevill Dysart Plantagenet Tollemache-Tollemache who lived at Tauranga on the North Island. His son, named simply Archibald Douglas, also lived in New Zealand, and in 1935 married Edna May Willis of Napier.

143

present generation, honouring those kindnesses shown to
Moses in Dublin so many years before.

NOTE TO THE TEXT

It is interesting to note that William Parker junior was alive in 1927 when
he gave an interview revealing many details of his parents' early days in
New Zealand. Much of this information is also included in the excellent
Petticoat Pioneers by Miriam Macgregor published by A.H. Reed in New
Zealand in 1973.

Chapter IX
London

Following the upheaval and emotion of Miriam and her family's departure for New Zealand, Moses moved to London, and whilst there, for a period of three years, he devoted most of his time to preaching, and to feverish literary activity, continuing his work on the Hebrew Old Testament, and writing his only work of fiction: *The Curates of Riversdale*,[1] which he curiously dedicated to that aloof Lord Mandeville whom he had met with the Duke and Duchess of Manchester in Paris in 1847. William Drogo Montagu had by now succeeded his father and was the Seventh Duke, and Moses obviously considered a light work of fiction was suitable for his Lordship's recommended reading. The three volumes were published in 1860. The work is a humorous satire on Anglicanism, and clearly contains quite an element of autobiography, thinly disguised, as are some of the characters. At the outset he quotes, with tongue in cheek, the Duke of Wellington: 'I should like to tell the truth, but if I did, I should be torn in pieces, here and abroad.' There is indeed a dangerous level of truth in *The Curates of Riversdale*. Real life people, such as Dr Pusey, and Dr Whateley, the fearsome Archbishop of Dublin, intermingle with the rest of the cast.

The character who tells the story is one of the curates –

---

[1] Published by Hurst and Blackett, 13 Great Marlborough Street, London.

the Revd George Holdsworth, and Riversdale is a 'town in the north of England' – no doubt Liverpool with perhaps a dash of Manchester. George possesses the sort of background that Moses admired, and at times coveted. 'I am the fourth of six sons of a Devonshire family,' he tells the reader, and on his mother's side he is distantly related to the wife of the Bishop of Kilcurragh, who lives in style on his estate just outside Dublin. The bishop is 'aristocratic, but not a vestige of pride is discernible in his bearing.' George goes to stay with his lordship, enjoying the festivities and the riot of parties that go on in the large house. It is all great fun, and no doubt reflects to some extent the social life of which Moses was a part during his time at TCD and Glasnevin. George returns to England and is ordained; he is happily married, comfortably off, and even visits North Africa where he and his wife meet up with a Mr Pferdkaufer, working as a missionary for the Church of Scotland – 'the English having found him too unmanageable!' (He was pulling his friend, Nathan Davis' leg.) The real Moses Margoliouth, however, is hidden behind the character of the Revd Monteleone, a converted Jew. About him, one of his fellow-clerics says: 'Do not encourage Jewish converts after ye have baptised them for fear they should become proud; keep them under.' Moses had clearly been well aware of feelings about him in certain quarters. Monteleone is described as 'almost an infidel; he crept up the sleeve of that Bishop of Kilcurragh and is made Rector of Ballytolka and examining chaplain to his Lordship.' Down the years Moses had never forgotten these slurs, and was now determined to strike back: 'The beggarly Jew is now too proud… we will bring him down yet and clip his wings. I dined the other day with a dear Irish brother-clergyman, Didimus O'Nihil, and he said before a score of brethren that it can be proved that Monteleone has intentions of eloping with a governess of his parish.' This is

sure proof that Moses was, over the years, at the receiving
end of cruel jibes, and he intended that some of those who
had mocked him should find themselves in print receiving
similar treatment. He alluded to the 'melancholic development of the vicar of Brimstone,' (Braintree – hinting at his
problems there), and the 'quarrels of Fowl Bentsneak, vicar
of Palenettle, with his parishioners.' He hints at the 'trials
and persecutions and malicious libels to which the Revd
Moshelleh Bargershon was subject' again a small vignette of
autobiography with which the book is sprinkled. It was his
one and only attempt at fiction, and although a comedy of
clerical life, there are more than hints of bad times endured
as well as good times enjoyed in the course of his journeys
and in the society of his friends.

He was by now living at 25 Great Russell Street,
Bloomsbury, and apart from his writing, he was preaching
and helping out in various London parishes. On 20th May,
he preached in St James' Upper Edmonton, at the instiga-
tion of D.J. White Esq., principal of the College-House
school there. He urged upon his youthful congregation the
importance of Christian witness and the need for missionary work. This was always a favourite topic. He pointed out
to them the miraculous effect of the Gospel on his own life,
hoping that they would come under the same influence –
'so that, after you will have left College-House, you may
carry the principles which you have learned there to your
homes present and past.'

On 17th December, 1860, he wrote a letter to the
Librarian of the British Museum (now the British Library):
'Finding that several of my smaller publications have not
found their way into the Library of the British Museum, I
take therefore the earliest opportunity to supply the
deficiency, by sending you the accompanying pamphlets.'
This was no doubt prompted by the archivist in him, and
the hope that his writings would be preserved for posterity.

*

It is depressing to discover the number of parishes which have amalgamated, and church buildings made redundant, over the last hundred and fifty years, and most of this ecclesiastical trauma has actually been condensed into the last half century. Added to this are the many vicarages and rectories which have passed out of the possession of the Church of England – some of the finest residences in the country, and so often replaced by what is second rate and unworthy. Perhaps more tragic is the fact that most Anglican clergymen now seem quite happy in their modern humdrum homes. Even Bishops can occasionally be heard to complain about their historic palaces, revealing that pedestrian taste has risen as high as the episcopacy. In this climate it is perhaps no wonder that the Church has also, in parishes up and down the land, discarded that liturgy which Moses considered to be so precious.

Moses moved to Wyton, near Huntingdon, a little before September, 1861, and was there for almost exactly twelve months.[2] He took a batch of christenings on 18th April, 1862: Frederick and Charles Leach, and Sarah and Emma Unwin. It seems that he was by then assuming the bulk of the work in the parish. History was repeating itself. His Vicar, perhaps unwell at the time, was the Revd Joseph Timothy Parker who died in that same year (1862), so it is quite possible that for the whole of the time Moses served at Wyton, he was taking on most of the burden of the parochial duties. Miriam was now of course safely in New Zealand, but Moses still had the responsibility of his son Charles. In an interesting flashback to his days in Dublin, he took up his pen and wrote to the Rt Hon. Sir Thomas

---

[2] What used to be the parish church there – a fine old church with a spire – is now derelict and in the hands of developers.

Fremantle, whom he had met at Glasnevin House. The letter is quoted in full:

> I humbly trust that you will kindly pardon the purport of this communication.
>
> I am in a strait and I am told that you may be the means, under God, of helping me. Having had once the honour of meeting you, about fifteen years ago, at the house of the late Bishop of Kildare, I venture to hope that you will take into favourable consideration the purport of this letter.
>
> I have a son, in his eighteenth year, he writes a good hand, and is generally intelligent. Unfortunately, I am too poor at present to support him. I have spent my all, and more, in the preparation of a great work, of which the enclosed is a Prospectus. My stipend from my Curacy – that of Wyton – is barely sufficient to provide me with the common necessaries of life; I have advertized (sic) for a couple of gentlemen to read with for Holy Orders but hitherto I have met with none.
>
> I am told that you might be able to find my son employment in HM Customs as an extra clerk. If such should be the case you would confer a most substantial favour on a very poor Clergyman, who has devoted all his time and energy to the service of his Church.
>
> I have taken the liberty of fowarding (sic) to you by this post, a copy of a little work, which I have just published, on the 'Essays and Reviews'.[3].
>
> I am, sir, Your most obedient servant,
> *M Margoliouth*

---

[3] The book he sent was *The End of the Law; being a Preliminary Examination of the Essays and Reviews* (Published 1861).

It appears from the above that no further funds were being sent to him from Suwalki; it is of course possible that by now his mother too had died and there is an implication that this was a low point in Moses' life. No archival material appears to exist which might confirm whether Sir Thomas saw fit to help, and in any case it was soon after this date that Charles decided that his prospects in England were poor leading to his decision to join his sister in New Zealand. Meanwhile for two years or so Moses continued preaching, writing and helping out with parish work on a freelance basis.

In the early part of 1863 he did a short spell as a locum in the parish of Offord Darcy, some three miles south of Huntingdon. The Prince of Wales was due to be married to Alexandra of Denmark on 10th March, and on the Sunday before, true to form, Moses preached a sermon in Offord Darcy church to celebrate the event. As usual he included a dedication, this time to the rector of the parish, the Revd William Thornhill, MA, 'as a grateful memento of the temporary spiritual oversight of your parish which you entrusted to my care.' He took as his text the eleventh verse of the third chapter of the Song of Solomon: 'Go forth, O ye daughters of Zion, and behold king Solomon with the crown wherewith his mother crowned him in the day of his espousals, and in the day of the gladness of his heart.' He pointed out that most weddings were humble affairs for private celebration when relatives and friends were invited to attend and witness, but it was appropriate, in the case of a member of the royal family, for the whole nation to rejoice. There was no truer patriot, and he reminded the congregation of the country's good fortune in possessing such a noble Queen and her offspring. When the reigning monarch is a despot and tyrant, the people cannot rejoice at the time of weddings and coronations. He quoted the throne of

150

Naples – ruled over by Ferdinand II with 'whips and scorpions.' He went on, 'But he is dethroned and has his just reward!' The Prince of Wales, he told them, had been nurtured and trained by his parents, and 'our hearts throb with affectionate solitude.' He then proudly mentioned that he had followed the life of His Royal Highness from the font to the altar and quoted the Hebrew poem he had written whilst at Trinity College, Dublin, and gave them a free translation. It was another opportunity for him to declare the proud allegiance he felt towards his adopted nation.

In February, 1864, he preached in All Saints, Huntingdon for the rector there, the Revd F. Gerald Vesey MA, and as so often over the years, he arranged for the text to be printed and the sales to be donated – on this occasion towards the installation of a pulpit in the nearby parish church of Hartford. Then, a little later in the same year, Moses was appointed Assistant Minister in the parish of St Paul's, Haggerston (in London's east end), working under the Revd William Stone, MA.[4] It was a milestone in his life, and it is probable that, from the pastoral point of view, he was now to perform his greatest work. It was as if his conversion all those years ago in Liverpool had been preparing him for this testing challenge. He both liked and respected his vicar, and the feeling was mutual. He wrote at this time: 'I find in my present worthy incumbent (William Stone) a true, sympathising, generous, tender-hearted Christian friend and brother,' and this relationship was to continue throughout his time there. Significantly he added, 'But I have known to my cost and sorrow a couple of different rectors, and am not alone in the experience of the unhappy past.' For most of the years he served at

---

[4] Formerly vicar of Butterton, Staffordshire, coincidentally not far from Wybunbury.

Haggerston, he lived at 26 Cambridge Terrace, Broke Road, Dalston.

By a strange coincidence one Ezekiel Margoliouth, a missionary, and his family, were then living nearby, in Bethnal Green. Ezekiel was also from Suwalki – it is surely probable that they were related, albeit distantly – but according to the archives of the CMJ there was no family connection. Ezekiel was the son of Abraham Margoliouth who had been chief Rabbi in Suwalki for thirty-three years, and his son, after converting to Christianity, worked for many years for the CMJ in London's Palestine Place. Moses became very close to his namesake, and this bond of friendship became stronger during his time in London. Unlike Moses, Ezekiel was never ordained. He was not a popular preacher, but was a Hebrew scholar of some repute.[5]

On 23rd October, 1864, he preached in St Paul's a Harvest Thanksgiving sermon which he dedicated to the organist, Lorenzo Edlington Mawer, and his choir.[6] Interestingly there had been recent mutterings amongst the parishioners that too much emphasis was being placed on the choral aspect of worship. Moses was never one to take attacks of this sort lying down, and he tackled the criticism head-on, taking on the role of St George on behalf of the beleaguered organist and his choristers. 'If you don't approve of church music,' he thundered, 'blame David, Solomon, Isaiah and St John!'

In the mid-1860s, Abyssinia was very much in the news, and in 1867 Moses organised a series of monthly missionary lectures to be delivered in the New Infants' School, Haggerston. The intention was to raise money to be put towards obtaining the release of the British Consul there,

---

[5] See also Appendix VI.
[6] The text was printed at Palestine Square.

152

Captain Charles Cameron, together with several missionaries, who were being held hostage. Most, perhaps all, of
the missionaries were working for the CMJ, so the whole
affair was causing considerable consternation in Palestine
Place. The Coptic Christian Emperor Tewodros II of
Abyssinia (known by the British as Theodore), had sought
military aid from Britain in order to attack his Moslem
neighbours. His request had been sent direct to Queen
Victoria, but the Foreign Office had refused to reply, and
Theodore immediately took prisoners in retaliation.
Neither funds nor diplomacy met with any success, until
finally the Tory Government under Lord Derby and
Disraeli ordered a military campaign. The whole operation
was meticulously planned, and some twenty thousand
Anglo-Indian troops were despatched from Bombay under
General Sir Robert Napier. As a result of a battle at Arogee,
just short of Magdala, the fortress home of Theodore, the
hostages were freed and the Emperor committed suicide.

During these years, although his time was much occupied with pastoral duties, he maintained his interests in
historical and archaeological matters. Late in 1869 he
delivered a lecture in Bury St Edmunds, which he later
published in January 1870. It was entitled 'The Vestiges of
the Historic Anglo-Hebrews in East Anglia'. He read the
paper before a meeting of the Royal Archaeological Institute
for Great Britain and Ireland. In it he attempted to trace
Jewish history in East Anglia from early times, giving
particular study, in view of the venue, to the antiquities in
Bury St Edmunds, and giving an account of the early
settlement of Jews in that part of the world. He alluded to
the Jewish brethren who had settled there, and argued that
many of them believed that Judaism, in its true sense,
involved the acceptance of Christianity. He was naturally
on to a favourite topic, and then, expanding into archaeology, he discussed the precise use of an ancient bronze

vessel which had once belonged to the synagogue in Bury St Edmunds.

Late in January, 1870, he received news from Paris that Chaja had died there on the 22nd. Her death occurred early that morning at the home of the Goldberg family – No. 3, Rue de Birague, in the quatrième arrondissement of the city. She was described as the wife of the missionary, Moses Margoliouth, and it was stated that she had been born in 1818 in Nouvelle Ville, the French for Neustadt, which in turn was the Prussian name for Wladyslawow, her home town in Poland where she and Moses had been married those many years before. One of the signatures on her death certificate was 'Louis aged 26', and described as 'brother of the deceased.'

So poor Chaja had been living in the French capital with, and under the protection of, her family. Hearing of her death, it is impossible to speculate on Moses' feelings; he cannot have felt great grief, but he must surely have dropped a tear of sympathy and have reflected on the old days in Poland, Liverpool and Dublin. Both Chaja's parents outlived her; her mother Rachel (née Silvermann) died in 1874, and the death of her father Bernard, a writer (described as *homme de lettres*), took place in 1886. Moses' father-in-law's full name was Baer Ben Alexander Goldberg. He had been born near Warsaw in 1799, and in due course achieved some eminence as a writer, often using the literary acronym 'Bag'. His parents died when he was young and in consequence he suffered much poverty in his youth, but managed to achieve an advantageous marriage, and settled in Wladyslawow. Shortly after Chaja's marriage there, the Goldbergs left Poland and settled in Berlin for a while before coming to London in 1847, where 'Bag' worked as a translator, possibly obtaining work with the help of his son-in-law. With her family now in England, it was probably at this time, coinciding with Moses leaving

Dublin, that Chaja returned to live with her parents. In 1852, the family finally settled in Paris. Chaja's father published a number of books and contributed articles on Jewish history and literature to a range of Hebrew periodicals.

Moses would of course have given Miriam and Charles the news of their mother's death, and no doubt they all felt sadness at what was the end of an era in all their lives. Importantly it brought, for Moses, a change in status. He was now a widower, and although her loss cannot have affected him greatly, it was a depressing time for him, and 1870 was a year in which he was very conscious of unfulfilled ambition. Throughout his life he endured such moments. His letter of ten years earlier to the British Museum was no doubt written in a spasm of frustration – it should be remembered that ambition, as well as Chaja, had driven him from Suwalki. Now, in 1870, he was getting nowhere with his Hebrew Old Testament. It was still as he had earlier complained, 'mouldering in manuscript, and likely to remain so for an indefinite period.' He now also wrote, somewhat pathetically, 'It has cost me so much in health, wealth and strength.' Also in a letter of 1870 to his friend, Revd W.J.C. Lindsay,[7] grandson of his old patron the Bishop of Kildare, he said, 'The chequered vicissitudes of my life, which you know too well, have thrown my name in the background.' But in fact the 1870s were to be a decade of excitement, change and success for him. Indeed it was to be a decade of excitement for the whole country. A mysterious death and the sexual scandals of the Bravo affair were to hold the nation enthralled for weeks on end. In 1871 Darwin would publish *The Descent of Man* causing more doubt and consternation to provoke the minds of the devout. The activities of the Prince of Wales were to set

---

[7] Then Rector of Llanvaches in the diocese of Llandaff.

tongues a-wagging, and, to Moses' delight, the conservative Disraeli would again become the country's Prime Minister from 1874 to 1880 and in 1876 his beloved Queen would become Empress of India. Above all, for Moses himself, the blurred melancholy of his private life was, in 1874, to be transformed into bright focus – he was to fall in love and marry, and in 1877 was destined to settle down in the peace of the Buckinghamshire countryside, far from the bustle and excitement of London.

As the months of 1870 drew on, matters already started to improve for him. In September 1870, he was appointed editorial secretary of a committee dedicated to organising a revision of the English Bible by Hebrew Christians.[8] The following month, on 4th October, he had the honour of being requested by the members to preach a sermon in St Saviour's Church, Forest Hill, London, which he entitled, 'The Oracles of God and their Vindication.' It was a particularly important occasion for him as it was the committee's inaugural address, and it was vital that the project should be given a good start. To have been asked to perform this duty was certainly an indication of the respect in which he was held. He told them that the production of his own edition of the Hebrew Bible had been one of the principal objects of his life, and that he had diligently studied the writings of Moses and the prophets in their original tongue with a view to their elucidation, and of course this new revision of the English Bible was to be based on the sort of scholarship for which he was well

---

[8] This eventually resulted in the Revised Version of the Bible, the New Testament being published first, in 1881. By July 1884, the Old Testament was added, thus enabling the Revisers to 'bring their long task to a close'. Although Moses did not manage to complete his own Hebrew edition (causing him 'illness, misfortune and disappointments') the Revised version stands as a monument to him and to the rest of the Committee, for their long years of scholarship and inspiration.

known. 'During my various travels,' he told them, 'in the east, the west and the north, I have ever borne in mind my great enterprise, viz. the illustration of the Scriptures of Truth.' He had, he explained, discovered a considerable number of new readings which would make many passages hitherto obscure, clear and intelligible.

He also gradually came to feel that his work in Haggerston was over, and early in the decade, he at last left St Paul's, and moved to the fashionable west end of the city, to take up a similar post in the parish of St Paul's, Onslow Square. By July 1872 he had moved across London, and had come to live at No. 22 Pelham Crescent, South Kensington, and during his time there he served under the vicar, the Revd C.D. Marston.[9] Moses and Charles Marston worked well together on various projects and it was probably Marston's death in 1876 which led to Moses' decision to leave. During his few years in this parish, which differed so widely from Haggerston, the 'Oakley Mission' was formed. This enlightened arrangement had been brought about by two neighbouring Chelsea parishes being excessively busy and over-populated. St Paul's took over a section of the Chelsea area in 1874: this addition did not become part of the Onslow Square parish, but was affiliated to it. The Oakley Rooms, which gave the Mission its name, were situated in Manor Street and, interestingly had originally been built in the 1850s in order to store military supplies for the Crimean War, which had been looming up those years ago when Moses was in Turkey in 1848. By a lucky chance this useful property, ideal for the purpose, came on the market just at the right time, and the parish was able to buy it and fit it out as a small chapel and mission room. Inevitably the situation led to some friction with their

---

[9] The author's father served as curate at St Bridget's, West Kirby, under the Revd Canon Stewart Jasper Marston, a kinsman of Charles Dallas Marston.

neighbours in Chelsea, but on the whole the idea proved a good one, and the arrangement lasted until 1904. Also during Moses' time there, a church hall and meeting room were built, all helping to cope with demands of what had become an unusually busy parish.

During his time at Onslow Square, he came to know Edmond and Eliza Beales, who lived at Osborne House, Bolton Gardens South, South Kensington.[10] Edmund Beales was an interesting character. He was born in 1803 and died in 1881. After Eton and Trinity College, Cambridge, he graduated in 1828 and was called to the Bar, Middle Temple, in 1830. His speciality became Equity Law and conveyancing, but he particularly came to know Moses through his connection with the Polish Exiles' Friends Society. Being President of the Reform League in 1866 at the time of the Hyde Park riots in July, he was involved in much controversy. His career advanced in 1870 when he was appointed a County Court Circuit Judge. His views were radical, but there is no evidence to show that Moses shared his desire to agitate for a further extension of the franchise; naturally the judge viewed with scorn and no doubt fury those members of parliament who were tempted to enter the political Cave of Adullam. Moses however much enjoyed the friendship and society of the Beales

---

[10] Near the home of the Potter family. On 19th May, 1883, Beatrix Potter wrote: 'No thrushes about here this spring, not seen tom-tits for a long time. I fancy two wrens about, cock been singing all winter. Two pairs of starlings, one pair from Mrs Crabb's garden, other Mr Beales. Been very busy getting worms for their young this long time.' And then later the same day: 'There is a pair of chaffinches in Mr Beales' garden.' On Monday, 28th May, 1883: 'The starlings are fledged. The swallows have disappeared, I am afraid they have not built here. There is a fine thrush for singing in Mr Beales' garden, he has some blackbird's notes in the middle of his song.' The judge died in 1881, but his widow lived on and, to Miss Potter, the garden would still be 'Mr Beales'; maybe his son lived there.

family in the comfort and luxury of their home in Kensington. This friendship was soon to be helpful in yet another of Moses' cherished endeavours.

Chapter X
Last Years

1874 brought joy and contentment of a kind which he had decided would be forever denied him. It is not known when he first met Sarah Smith, widow, of 13 Onslow Crescent, but they fell in love, and were married on 14th October in the Parish Church of Holy Trinity, Brompton.[1] She brought him great happiness, and a few years later he was to describe her, in a private letter, as 'God's most precious gift to me.' (If evidence were needed, this is further proof of the unsatisfactory nature of that first marriage in Wladyslawow). Sarah Golding St Osyth Smith, née Golding, was born in London in 1827, the daughter of Benjamin Golding. She was a widow, but appears to have had no children. She had at least two married sisters, and numerous nephews and nieces. As her name implies, she was no doubt descended from the Golding family of St Osyth, near Clacton-on-Sea in Essex – there are several Golding memorials in the churchyard there – and she brought to the marriage not only happiness, but also, to a modest degree a financial security which Moses had not enjoyed for over twenty years. (It is possible as her name suggests, that she came from Jewish stock, but this is not certain.)

Meanwhile Moses continued with his pastoral work in

---

[1] St Paul's, Onslow Square, is now incorporated into the Holy Trinity parish.

London until, late in 1876, an opportunity presented itself – he was offered the living of Little Linford near Newport Pagnell in Buckinghamshire. The squire of the parish was Matthew Knapp who lived in nearby Little Linford Hall, just a short step from the church, dedicated to St Leonard. Perhaps the Knapp family had a town house in the vicinity of Onslow Square, or maybe Moses' new wife was a close friend of theirs – she could well have been distantly related to them; it is certainly very possible that Moses came to be offered the living through Sarah. What is sure is that Matthew Knapp had this small and attractive living in his gift, and he had just had a vicarage built the previous year (1875) to house the new incumbent and his wife.[2] With the death of Charles Marston, Moses had that much less to keep him in London, and he seized the chance of moving out into the tranquil countryside of rural Buckinghamshire. Moses was inducted into the living on 30th January, 1877, by the Bishop of Oxford, and there he was destined to live, quietly and happily for those few years remaining to him. Happy for sure, as he was now to share the rest of his life with his dearest Sarah. The vicarage was roomy, and big enough for the Margoliouths to house two servants, both local girls – Matilda Gaskins and Rose Caroline King.

Little Linford was perfect for him. The attractive countryside, the idyllic setting of the beautiful small fourteenth century church (in early days a Chapel of Ease to Tickford Abbey in nearby Newport Pagnell), the proximity of his friends and patrons the Knapp family, and a peaceful

---

[2] In the 'History and Antiquities of the Newport Hundreds' (c. 1900) by Oliver Ratcliff, the vicarage is described as 'pleasantly situated about half a mile to the north east of the church. It was erected through the influence of the late Arthur and Matthew G.S. Knapp. The two gentleman also gave the amount of four thousand pounds to the church for ever. This sum is invested and the income amounts to £128 per annum.'

domestic life – all this formed a perfect background to his final years. The persecution, the jealousies he had endured long ago were now of little account. Such incidents as the furore at Tranmere, and those last few miserable weeks at Wybunbury, could be discarded and forgotten. There had been good times and many achievements, and he could remember them with satisfaction as he carried out his work in the small parish. His preaching, ever an attraction, soon filled the small church to capacity, and again he was able to demonstrate his undoubted charm and charisma in yet another corner of the Lord's vineyard, and now with the support of a loving wife.

In 1878, his first full year at Little Linford, two more matters figured dramatically in his life. The first brought him much satisfaction, and went some way to fulfil that dream which he had held since those very early years of his conversion. His nephew George, son of his brother Herschel, had been studying on the continent, in Dusseldorf and at the University of Bonn, and following in the footsteps of his uncle, he had also become a convert to Christianity. He had recently arrived in England, and in April Moses baptised him in Little Linford church. He became almost a son to Moses and Sarah, and was soon to be ordained and pursue a brilliant career.[3]

In the same year, Moses prophetically published an important lecture which he entitled 'The Destinies of Israel'. Even though he was now a Church of England country parson, he never lost the love and care he felt for his fellow Jews and the Nation of his birth. On 26th June this talk was delivered before an influential audience in the Kensington drawing room of his friends Edmond and Eliza Beales, who at Moses' request, had lent their home for the occasion. The theme of the lecture was the need for a homeland to be

---

[3] See Appendix V.

found for the Jewish Nation. 'Surely,' he told them, 'you will consider the little vicar of Little Linford beside himself in attempting to solve such a problem.' He pointed out that the Jews were a people weak and small, without a king, (in his opinion a big handicap), and who had lost their political status two thousand years ago. But no nation on earth was more deserving of a land of her own. Disraeli, he complained, had done nothing, and neither had Bismarck, and pressure should be brought to bear on the leading nations of the world to achieve this desired goal. 'Even the recent remarkable discoveries of nature and science,' he told them, 'do not diminish my belief in the destiny of the House of Jacob'. In the light of modern history, it was an interesting gesture, far-sighted and ambitious, and to be momentously achieved just seventy years later.

Both Miriam and Charles remained distant figures, but they continued to communicate, and he received news from time to time of their pioneering life in New Zealand. In an entirely different way they had done what Moses had dared to do in 1837. Charles fades from the scene, his communications becoming less and less as the years slipped by. William and Miriam certainly remained in touch, relaying details of their hardship and tragedy along with their lucky escape in 1868. Their little daughter Helen, only nine months old, had died in 1867. Their first-born Minnie, the young heroine of the Poverty Day massacre, died of diphtheria on 29th April, 1875 aged only twenty, and their son Frank also died a year later on 28th April, 1876, aged seventeen. But their sons William Junior (b. 1857), Frederick (b. 1861) and John (b. 1868) together with their parents, formed the Parker family at the time when Moses and Sarah were at Little Linford in the late 1870s.

In February 1881, Moses went to London. He had been asked to give a private talk on Jewish history, and at the same time he was arranging for the publication of what was to be his last work: *Some Triumphs and Trophies of the Light of the World*, (1882). He was staying at the Portland Hotel in Great Portland Street, when he suddenly suffered a heart attack. He was ill for three days, but nothing could be done, and he died in the presence of his nephew George who had been in London at the time. It was the 25th February, 1881.[4]

This, for Sarah, must have been a terrible shock, and George was left to make arrangements for the funeral, which took place in Little Linford church, back home in the parish where he had been so happy for too short a period.

Not only was Sarah devastated, the whole parish was in mourning. To quote from the Guardian of 9th March, 1881:

A clergyman of special note as a learned Hebraist and Oriental and Talmudical scholar died almost suddenly of heart disease on February 25th. He was an earnest, able, and energetic worker among his own people, and his great Rabbinical and Talmudical learning gave him access to many of the more highly educated Jewish families, and one of the converts whom he won, by God's blessing, from amongst them is now a student at Cuddesdon, and will shortly be ordained. He was buried on Ash Wednesday in the churchyard of the quiet little country parish, Little Linford, near Newport Pagnell, where he had been vicar since 1877. How he was valued by the neighbouring clergy, and how he had endeared himself to

---

[4] For students of coincidence: a subscriber to Moses' first publication was the Revd A. Ayling of Guildford. It will be remembered that the one body identified after the loss of the 'Avenger' *was S. Ayling*, as per the name in marking ink on the shirt. The signature clearly visible on Moses' death certificate is that of A.H.W. Ayling LSA (Licentiate of the Society of Apothecaries).

164

his parishioners, from the squire, who is patron of the living, to the poorest of the people, was manifest by the attendance of, as it seemed, the whole of the parish, first at Holy Communion at noon, and then at the funeral at 3 p.m. The celebration and subsequent service were taken, at his widow's request, by the Revd S. J. Stone, vicar of St Paul's, Haggerston, the son of a venerable and saintly clergyman under whom Dr Margoliouth worked for several years in the East of London.

It was a token of the esteem in which he had been held during his time at Haggerston that the son of his dear friend William Stone was asked to take the service and preach the sermon. A short account was given of his early days, and special mention was made of his joy in baptising his nephew. Samuel John Stone[5] alluded to Moses' recent connection with the 'Parochial Mission to the Jews Fund,' which had been established 'to supply curates especially trained to work in large parishes where Jews abound.' (It was by then an institution well established, and was supporting funds in both Leeds and London). Mr Stone continued: 'The gifted tongue has lost its power of utterance. It had been the interpreter of thought in many lands and many languages, not given in a moment by inspiration, but painfully and diligently acquired. He could speak, and he rejoiced to speak, of the wonderful works of God, as the Spirit gave him utterance, with wonderful correctness and accuracy, if we may judge by the facility with which he expressed himself in our own language – the country of his adoption – so difficult it is to acquire. That also is still and silent… according to the will of God.

---

[5] He had succeeded his father as vicar of St Paul's Haggerston in 1874. He was a graduate of Pembroke College, Oxford, and was ordained in 1862.

'These walls which were soon found to be all too narrow, testify to the value in which his ministrations were held. It became necessary soon to 'enlarge the place and lengthen the cords,' and we are surrounded by signs and tokens which tell us how well he loved 'the habitation of the Lord's House, and the place where His honour dwelleth.' As a clergyman, I can speak with the warmest consciousness of the loss which I have personally sustained by his removal. The same expressions of universal regret are spoken on all sides, for he was, in truth, a ready helper, prepared to advocate his Master's cause, in the pulpit or on the platform – willing, at any call that reached him, to go amongst his neighbour's people, as much at home in a parish-school room as at a Congress of the Church, and especially if he might speak on that subject which filled his heart.'

Addressing particularly the parishioners of Little Linford, he went on, 'We have seen him and known him for four short years, during which he has dwelt in the presence of us all, familiar and accessible, courteous and kind to the least and to the greatest. A smile, a kind word, a thoughtful inquiry, letting one know that out of sight with him was not out of mind: these acts of kindness... have won their way amongst us, inspiring a sentiment of universal respect and esteem, growing, as the circle of acquaintance became closer and nearer, into affection and love.'

Also at the time of his death, and recognising how dear Little Linford had been to him, a few lines were written in his memory by 'a dear young friend':

A tranquil haven there to cease
From tumult for a few sweet years;
Foreshadowing the perfect peace
Of the bright mansion God prepares.

It was the end of a long journey, at times wearying, and at times requiring the rare nerve and resolution which he certainly possessed. It must surely be true that he had, for the most part, enjoyed life, and he had both given and received much. His learning, especially in Hebrew and Jewish history, was unquestioned, but he was at the same time an entertaining man; a sparkling character. Congregations in his hands, soon, from 'a few tens' would become 'as many hundreds.' He was always immensely proud of being Jewish, but at the same time he maintained a fearless opposition to his own people when it came to his belief in the Christian Creed, and would vehemently defend his conversion. On this point he never wavered and his enthusiasm remained undimmed. He was as aware as any of his race of the tragic dispersal of the Jews following the destruction of the first Temple at Jerusalem. In the face of persecution Jews have learnt to survive as a scattered but necessarily combined force, and Moses was a shining example of that loyalty and cohesion. His obituary in the Jewish World of 4th March, 1881, was inevitably biased:

DEATH OF DR MARGOLIOUTH. The death is announced, at the age of 60, of the Revd Moses Margoliouth, MA, LL.D., Vicar of Little Linford, Newport Pagnell, Bucks, one of the revisers of the English version of the Old Testament. The deceased, who was of foreign Jewish extraction, became a convert of Christianity in early manhood, and after studying under the late Dr A. M'Caul, entered Trinity College, Dublin. After passing the curriculum there he was admitted to Holy Orders. This Dr Margoliouth, like all converts, had throughout his career to display redoubled efforts in order to endeavour to convince his patrons of his earnestness in the cause of Christianity, which he professed to take up. His arduous labours must therefore have been a great strain on his weak body, but his masters were nevertheless exacting, and still demanded incessant exertions in seeking new converts from his ancestral faith.

He would have dismissed this cynical assessment. It was typical of many of the brickbats which he endured during his life; the diligence with which he performed his pastoral duties was proof to the contrary. From that memorable day in 1837 until the day he died, he had maintained an unswerving adherence to his faith.

From that very first weekend in Liverpool, he was fortunate with his friendships. Firstly and crucially he met the rather indistinct Mr Lazarus; then he came into contact with the Joseph/Leveaux clan; he had been helped by the kindly academic, Dr Alexander M'Caul – so useful during his London visits – perhaps, above all, there entered his life the timely and practical Ashton family of Tranmere. It must be said that the group all sharing Jewish ancestry, and so inter-related, was a truly amazing and accomplished crowd, and all, in their ways, faced challenge and change. Nathan and Catherine Davis had been there in Tunis, greeting him with open arms and battling against the odds in North Africa on behalf of the Church of Scotland. (Of course it cut both ways – how welcome Moses' visit must have been to them at the time). There was poor (literally) Henry Joseph, born in Bedford, lived in Norwich, came to Liverpool, then Chester; after losing his first wife he married for a second time, in Dublin, and eventually died alone and miserable in Strasbourg. Another friend was Samuel Asher Levi Herbert – again a remarkable life. Born in Colchester, he arrived in Liverpool, went on to TCD and ordination, followed by his Christian ministry in the north east, London, back to Gateshead, and eventually served as a parish priest in rural Devon. Also in Moses' circle was the Leveaux family; wine merchants, benevolent and consequential, whose undoubted kindnesses to the Margoliouth family were private and unrecorded. Bishop Samuel Gobat and his wife ('the Bishop and Bishopess'), had clearly been so hospitable to him during his stay in Jerusalem. Not least in this list were the aristocratic Lindsays headed by that kindly, wide-sleeved, Bishop, who had extended a hand of friendship and influence just when he needed it, and introduced him to a strata of society into which he fitted so comfortably, but which otherwise would have been barred to him. Added to this were so many characters, friends, parishioners, who admired and respected this curious and clever academic, with his odd European accent, in which he would recount his incredible tales of journeys abroad.

There were times in his life when his fellow-Jews perhaps could have shown, in the matter of apostasy, a little more charity; his loyalty to them occasionally deserved better. Neither does the Church of England emerge entirely unscathed from the story; the kindnesses of such as the Ashton family were not by any means emulated in every quarter. Too often came taunts to lacerate his Jewish heart. It must be said that Moses himself was no saint. His first marriage failed, and his children at times must have led a nomadic and rootless existence. There were moments in his life when only the unbelievable kindness and hospitality of his gang of friends enabled him to survive. The Ashtons of Tranmere deserve special mention. They, with their happy brood of children, could take Miriam and Charles into their enlarged family, and give them a share of their happiness. While Charles Ashton toiled as a city clerk, Moses could go a-travelling the world, and return home with tales of his amazing experiences. But it was the right way round: Moses, out-going, confident and charismatic, was the perfect one to take on the role of explorer and adventurer, preacher and raconteur.

A fortune had passed through his hands, but only as a means of following the star which had ever shone so brightly for him. The extravagance he showed in the matter of his two hobbies – travel and publishing – inevitably brought hardship on himself ('I am in a strait,' he had told Sir Thomas Fremantle), and this must have affected those dearest to him. On the other hand, others – presumably her own family – had taken on the responsibility of Chaja at No. 3, Rue de Birague. This had allowed Moses an independence which for so many years his way of life patently demonstrated. His failure to produce his Hebrew Bible was forever a disappointment, but it was nevertheless a department of scholarship to which he was able to contribute with distinction. In spite of the cruelty of some, he had been able to enjoy the friendship of many, and in his final years he must have looked back with great satisfaction on his tortuous, triumphant journey from a small, remote Polish town to a happy marriage in a country parsonage in one of the lovely shires of England. It was an incredible story, and as was observed in his lifetime, 'as astonishing and romantic as anything in Mr Disraeli's fictions'.

This short book may well encourage a little more light to be shed on the colourful, heroic life of the Reverend Dr Moses Margoliouth. On his tombstone beside the beautiful little church in Little Linford are, simply inscribed in both English and Hebrew, the words:

As for me, I will behold Thy face in righteousness: I shall be satisfied, when I awake, with Thy likeness.'

Psalm 17, verse 15

Postscript

Within a short time of his death, Moses Margoliouth was forgotten by all except those who had been closest to him. The interesting details of his life gathered dust, and have remain hidden for over a century. I hope the reader will consider that this story has been worth the telling. Sarah, in her will, left twenty-five pounds to Little Linford for an East Window in memory of her husband, and it is a fitting memorial.

Moses' nephew George (1853–1924) was ordained in 1881, the year of his uncle's death, and in due course made a name for himself in the field of Arabic scholarship.[1] He was educated at Dusseldorf, the University of Bonn, Cuddesdon College, Oxford, and Queen's College Cambridge. He wrote many books.

As for William and Miriam, it is perhaps significant, certainly proving that they kept in touch, that Sarah left Miriam a generous bequest in her will (two hundred pounds). Miriam was described in the document as 'my husband's daughter', and was then living in 'Fitzgerald Road, Napier, New Zealand'. She also left George two hundred pounds. To her numerous nephews and nieces, the children of her sisters, she left fifty pounds each. Their surnames were either Prater or Falkener. Miriam's husband William died aged seventy-one on 2nd July, 1894, and Miriam herself died on 10th July, 1913, 'aged 78', further confirmation of the year of her birth, 1835. After William's

---

[1] See also Appendix V.

death, she lived at 90 Milton Road, Napier. John died the following year, and Frederick and William junior lived on for some years. William was described as working as a clerk in the Crown Lands Office, Napier, in the Hawke's Bay Almanac of 1889, and Frederick had joined the staff of the Bank of New South Wales, being manager of the Gisborne branch from 1887 to 1915.

Charles is not mentioned in Sarah's will. He was presumably either dead by then or they had just failed to keep in touch, but he established something of a dynasty in the Napier and Gisborne areas of New Zealand, and there are Margoliouths still living there, including a Lindsay Margoliouth, serving as a reminder of Moses' close connection with the Lindsay family of Glasnevin House one hundred and fifty years ago.

Sarah left a silver loving cup to a member of the Knapp family, at least proving that in 1889, the date of the relevant codicil, their friendship was maintained.

After Moses' death, Sarah stayed on at the vicarage for a short period to sort things out, but as is the way of things she could not remain there long, and she took a house called Rougemont in Iffley, Oxford. She packed up her possessions, her clocks, her antiques, her family pictures, and moved there to live on for almost another nine years, latterly looked after by her servants, Harriett Crutch, Clara Bailey, Ellen Nagerdah, and Reeves – perhaps the gardener. After a short illness she died on 15th December, 1889, aged 63, and was buried with her husband in the Churchyard at Little Linford, in the shadow of its ancient church, in the small village where they had both been so happy. Above her name and the date of her death are inscribed the words:

'Blessed are the merciful.'

Appendix I
H.S. Joseph (1799–1864)

Henry Samuel Joseph, formerly Nathan Joseph, was a
senior member of that 'gang' of Christian Jews who were so
helpful to Moses Margoliouth during his early years in
England. He was born in Bedford on 13th August, 1799,
the second son of Michael Joseph of Bedford, silversmith.
In July, 1839, Henry Joseph married, his first wife being
Margaret Brown, widow of Michael Brown, and daughter
of John Brown, master mariner. Joseph took on four step-
children: Sarah b. 1818 (married Edward Henry Leveaux,
1849), Mary Eliza b. 1822, John (later Revd John Brown),
and Catherine b. 1825 (married Revd Nathan Davis in
1844). In 1841 Joseph became chaplain of the Workhouse,
49 Great Newton Street, Liverpool. His salary was then
fifty eight pounds per annum; by 1843 this had risen to two
hundred and fifty, and by then he was also working for the
C.M.J., being its representative in the north-west, centred
on Chester. By 1845 his health had deteriorated, and the
committee of the C.M.J. recorded at the time that they
'deeply regret that they have been deprived by his illness,
for many months past, of the valuable services of the Revd
H.S. Joseph.' May, 1846: 'The Revd H.S. Joseph, the state
of whose health has been such as for a considerable time, to
prevent his actively engaging in his duties, has resigned the
office of visitor of the Society's Associations. Your committee earnestly pray that by divine blessing his health may
be speedily and fully restored.' From 1847 to 1856 he was

Chaplain of Chester Gaol.

In November, 1847, he baptised in St Bride's Church, Chester, 'Miss H.R., a deeply interesting young Jewess,' according to the 'Jewish Intelligence' of February, 1848. She was probably his niece, Helena Rosenburg. At this time he was living at Rose Bank Cottage, Upton, near Chester. It seems that soon after this he moved into Chester town centre, living at Union Walk, in the parish of St John. On 15th May, 1849, he wrote to the Central Committee of the CMJ to say that Moses Margoliouth was the author of an anonymous circular. This seems to have been the subject of a temporary dispute between the two men. His wife died on 28th November, 1849, and in the 1851 census he was a widower, aged fifty, of 25 Union Walk. In 1855 he no longer appears as co-secretary of the CMJ auxiliary in Chester, and from 1852 there are no traces of his annual subscription. In 1856 he ceased to be chaplain of Chester Gaol. On 15th April, 1852 he re-married, his second wife being Frances Chapman, spinster, of Dalkey, Dublin, the wedding taking place in Monkstown Parish Church.

Interestingly H.S. Joseph published a small volume in 1853 entitled *Memoirs of Convicted Prisoners, accompanied by remarks on the Causes and Prevention of Crime*. It was published by Wertheim & Co., Paternoster Row, London, and was 'available at all the booksellers in Chester.' Joseph wrote this book during the time of his chaplaincy of Chester Castle (then the Gaol), and in the frontispiece is a print of the castle. He quotes a number of curious details of crimes committed in Cheshire and the north west, and points out the tragedy they cause, expressing a remarkably modern and humanitarian view. He quotes a letter sent by a convict he had known, who had been sent to Australia and eventually had been given permission to send for his wife. The convict wrote: 'My dear wife, this is quite a different country to old England. There is no such things as pawn shops; the woods abound with parrots and other birds of beautiful plumage. The water is good, and except two months in the year, July and August, it is all summer. Please come... Bring a few dozen pictures out as they are worth a great deal here, and silver watches which only cost ten shillings in England are worth fifty here.'

For some years Henry Joseph lived in Strasbourg, and some details of his last days emerged in a curious series of letters which appeared in the *Bedfordshire Times* in November 1875. One Morris Lissack of Bedford, an opponent of the CMJ, wrote to the paper to allude to a 'case of local interest'. He wrote, on 20th November: 'Having heard that the Revd Professor Marks, of the University College, London, had attended the deathbed of the so-called Revd Nathan Joseph (who was a native of this town, and was a celebrated missionary of his day, having attended periodically the Bedford meetings, as the deputation from the parent Society, being afterwards chaplain to Chester Gaol), I wrote to the Revd Professor for the particulars, and I extract the following from that gentleman's reply:

I stopped at the Villa de Paris Hotel, Strasbourg, on my way home from Switzerland. On the morrow after my arrival at the hotel, the waiter informed me that the chaplain of the hotel, who had seen my name in the list of new-comers, desired to see me in his room where he lay ill in bed. To my great astonishment the chaplain turned out to be the Revd N. Joseph whom I had known years before, as Chaplain of the Liverpool Infirmary, and whom I had not seen for nearly twenty-five years. He was then sinking from disease and did not appear to have many days life in him. He said that his object in requiring my presence was that he might extract from me a promise to see his remains after death brought over to 'pyver Jisroeil' – a Jewish burial. I absolutely refused to give such a promise., and I remarked that it puzzled me to conceive how one who had professed and taught Christianity should be so desirous of a Jewish burial. I then discovered what I had in Liverpool keenly suspected, that Joseph's confession of Christianity with his lips was no indication of the belief of his heart. As I declined to give him the promise he asked, he requested me to pray with him and to offer him consolation. I readily did so, and on the following morning I left Strasbourg whilst he was yet living. Since then I have never heard of him, nor do I know whether he is still in being.

Bedfordshire Times, 18th November, 1876: letter from Morris Lissack saying that Bedford people are cautious of some Jewish converts, and quoting specific cases:

Nor do they forget the cause why the Revd N. Joseph – referred to in my letter to the Chairman – was obliged to resign the honourable post of Chaplain to Chester Gaol through his dishonest proceedings.

Lissack continues in the same letter:

My Christian friends can hardly enter into the horror of my feelings when the baptised missionary, after his disgraceful conduct in Chester and Northampton, came to Bedford on his way to France, and preached in St Cuthbert's church. I felt it keenly that such a man should be allowed to enter a pulpit that had always been graced by men of piety and unimpeached character. I believe it was during the time when the

Revd Mr Trollope was the officiating clergyman, and who was universally beloved and respected by all who knew him.

Bedfordshire Times, 25th November, 1876: reply by John Barraclough, Association Secretary for the CMJ, to Mr Lissack's letter:

...I wish... the Professor had... been more prudent in the getting up of his case. It is a death-bed scene – at Strasbourg, hundreds of miles away – twelve or fifteen years ago – when none but himself and the dying man were present...

The Revd Henry Samuel Joseph clearly had a sad end; it is surely impossible to imagine that his life was the sham suggested by Mr Lissack and Professor Marks. Assuming there is any truth about his final request (as John Barraclough pointed out, there was then only one witness alive), his thoughts and wishes must have been caused by the influence of his final illness and a distressed mind.

Henry Joseph's 'disgraceful conduct' was debt.

Appendix II
Samuel Asher Levi Herbert (1818–1885)

Samuel Herbert was a close friend of Moses Margoliouth, and also a converted Jew. Born in Colchester in 1818, the son of Myer and Hannah Levi, later known as John and Hannah Herbert. His mother Hannah was the daughter of Michael Joseph of Bedford, and was sister to Nathan, later Henry Samuel Joseph, Moses' friend from Liverpool and Chester. Samuel Herbert was baptised by Henry Joseph on 10th September, 1837, just a few months before Moses' baptism. Later attended TCD. Graduated B.A., ordained, and was curate Sunderland, 1847–9 during the time Moses was away on his travels. Curate Gateshead, 1849–1858; Clerkenwell, 1858–1862; Gateshead, 1862–1864; Rector of St James's, Gateshead until 1881, and then Rector of Ashbury and North Looe, Exbourne, Devon, until his death in 1885. He published *The Apostle Paul, a model for Sunday School Teachers, after 1862;* and *Convocation, its present Constitution, 1868.*

He married Annie Jane Beresford Dolan, daughter of John Dolan, gent, and sister of the Revd J.A. Dolan, in Dublin on 13th March, 1851. His wife was born in Dublin c. 1829. They had a number of children, establishing quite a dynasty:

1. Emily Elizabeth Hannah, baptised Jan. 1852. Teacher.

Married 1880 Sir James Richard Thursfield. Their son was Rear Admiral Henry George Thursfield.

2. Jane Katherine, baptised Oct. 1853. Governess to Lord Joicey's family. (The Joiceys were coal owners of Gateshead; they lived in Chester-le-Street, Co. Durham.) She died 1939 at The Cottage, Falloden, Northumberland.

3. Annie Theodora, baptised Sept. 1855. Studied the piano in Berlin, and later became head of the family's school in Tynemouth. Died unmarried, Sidcup, Kent, 1928.

4. Mary Adelaide, baptised May, 1857. Trained at St Thomas' Hospital, and was later matron, Worcester Royal Infirmary. Died unmarried.

5. Robina Constance, born c. 1859. Was theatre sister at St Thomas' Hospital, and later housekeeper to her brother Henry at Berkhamstead and Falloden. Died unmarried.

6. Florence. Baptised c.1861.

7. John Alexander. Born 26 Aug., 1862. Attended Newcastle Royal Grammar School. Sizar, St John's College, Cambridge. Worked in the British Museum MSS Dept. and was finally Deputy Keeper, 1921–27. He became a Roman Catholic in 1909, and died in 1948. No doubt he would have known George Margoliouth. Wrote *Schools of Illumination; Illuminated MSS,* etc. Married 1896, Alice, daughter of Lt. Col. R. Aufrere Baker, R.A., and widow of Walter H. Low M.A. Their only child was Rose Beresford Herbert, who married Frederick Edward Godden.

8. Hilda. Born c. 1866. Nurse, trained at Carlisle. Died c. 1899.

9. Edward William. Born c. 1867. Attended Newcastle Royal Grammar School, and then Crediton School. Exhib. Jesus College, Oxford. Taught at the Edinburgh

180

Academy. Died unmarried, 1934, at Broadbury, Gullane, (E. Loth.)

10. Henry Beresford, born 1869. Newcastle Royal Grammar School; Leamington College. Exhib. Exeter College, Oxford. Housemaster Berkhamstead School. Became Private Secretary to Viscount Grey of Falloden. Chairman Alnwick District Council, and a J.P. 1934. Died unmarried, London, 1951.

11. Clara. Born c. 1872. Studied the piano at the Scharvenker School in Berlin. Married Frank Ainsworth Willcox. Their son was Frank Arthur Willcox, M.D.Cantab. and FRCP, died 1963 in Highgate. Their daughter Margaret Ainsworth, M.B. and B.Chir. Girton College, married Henry Norman Knox. There are several medical descendants.

In 1884, just before Samuel Herbert's death, his younger brother, George Henry Herbert, 'merchant', died in Newcastle-on-Tyne, unmarried, and left £2,070 to Samuel Herbert and his family.

Appendix III

Edward Henry Joseph Leveaux
Friend of Moses Margoliouth from c.1840

Edward Henry Leveaux was the son of Henry Leveaux, wine merchant, and his wife Catherine. Edward Leveaux also followed in his father's footsteps into the wine trade. (He was described as a 'wine agent'.) Edward was born in Bedford, c. 1828. His mother, Catherine (otherwise called Katherine or Kate) Joseph was the daughter of Michael and Esther Joseph, of Bedford, and sister to Nathan, later Henry Samuel Joseph. Henry Joseph was therefore Edward's uncle. The Leveaux family moved at some stage to Chester, probably in 1838, and lived there, in Union Walk, in St John's parish. It is likely that Henry Leveaux, the father, owned Rose Bank Cottage as well as the house in Union Walk, both in turn becoming home to his brother-in-law, the Revd Henry Samuel Joseph.

Henry Leveaux was clearly a man both prosperous and benevolent, and was the most likely person to have assisted Moses Margoliouth financially in 1840. On 26th April, 1849, not long before her mother's death, Sarah Brown, Henry Joseph's step-daughter, married Edward Leveaux. Uncle Henry Joseph took the wedding in St John's Church, Chester. Witnesses: Nathan Davis (he and his wife Catherine, sister of the bride, were by then back from Tunis), and Mary Eliza Brown, another of the bride's sisters. John Brown, later the Revd John Brown, who was at TCD during Moses' pilgrimage, was also present. He was brother of the bride. Edward and Sarah lived first at 16 Ivy Street, Birkenhead, and then moved to Tranmere, and presumably Henry Joseph then moved into the Union Walk house, round about the time he obtained his appointment as Chaplain to Chester Gaol.

Henry Leveaux almost certainly had some hand in arranging for Moses, on his return from Jerusalem, to take up the post of curate at St Catherine's, Tranmere. He died on 26th March, 1859, aged sixty-two, at Eldon House, Tranmere, where he was described as 'a jeweller and wine merchant'. By 1863 Edward Leveaux and his family had moved to London (Putney), and were still in touch with Moses, also by then in London. At some stage (perhaps c. 1875) Edward became a widower; he re-married, his second wife being Helena Rosenburg, Henry Joseph's niece (see Joseph appendix) who was born in York, c. 1835. Interestingly, Edward's brother Isidore (died Aug. 1886 at 194 Adelaide Road, Hampstead), was the father of Montague Leveaux, known professionally as Vivian Ellis, who enjoyed a successful career in the theatrical world. Edward and Catherine had a number of children:

1. Josephine (Kate), born Feb. 1850. Unmarried. Was living with her stepmother, Helena in Putney, in 1891, and died there in January 1937.
2. Adelaide Sarah. Born Chester, 1853. Became a Mrs Houghton.
3. Edward Henry. Born Chester, c. 1854.
4. Frederick. Born Rock Ferry, c. 1855.
5. Arthur M. Born Rock Ferry, c. 1859.
6. Constance E. Born Rock Ferry, c. 1860.
7. Alice, Born Putney, c. 1863.

Appendix IV
Court Martial

Court Martial held on board HMS Trafalgar in Malta Harbour on Monday 31st day of January, 1848 and continued by adjournment on Tuesday the first day of February, 1848.

Present:
Sir Lucius Curtis Bart., CB, Rear Admiral of the Fleet and Second Officer in the Command of Her Majesty's Ships and Vessels on the Mediterranean Station. President. (With six Captains)

The Court Martial was of Lieutenant Francis Rooke; Mr John Larcom, Gunner; William Hill, Captain's Steward; James Morley, Boy of the first Class, for their conduct upon the occasion of the wreck of Her Majesty's Steam Ship Avenger, Commanded by Captain Charles George Edward Napier, upon a Reef of Rocks or Shoal lying between the Island of Galita and the African Coast, at about 10 o'clock on the night of the 20th of December, 1847 – the said (names) being the only survivors of the Crew who were on board the said Vessel.

Abstracts from the Court's findings:
'...the precise cause of this sad disaster had not been shown in the evidence produced before the Court. But the Court is of the opinion that no blame whatsoever can be imputed

to the said (names) for their conduct upon the occasion and it doth therefore acquit the said (names) and the said (names) are hereby fully acquitted accordingly.

'And the Court is further of the opinion that the conduct of the said Lieut. Francis Rooke in lowering the Boats was proper, being in obedience to the Orders of his Captain, and that after the leaving of the Cutter in which he was, his perseverance in endeavouring to remain near the Wreck for the purpose of rendering assistance, until forced away by the violence of the weather, as well as his subsequent conduct in the boat under such perilous circumstances, and also in proceeding to Tunis to obtain assistance and again returning in search of the Wreck, was most officer-like and praiseworthy.'

The court also praised the '... manly and seamanlike conduct of Mr John Larcom, the Gunner, nor can it pass over in silence the humane and hospitable treatment the survivors received from the Arab herdsman who first administered to their necessities.'

'But the Court deems it necessary to state that the evidence produced leaves a doubt in the mind of the Court as to whether the Avenger had on board the usual Mediterranean Charts at the time of her Wreck.'

Appendix V

The Revd G. Margoliouth
Obituary: *The Times*, 17th May, 1924

The Revd George Margoliouth, who died on Wednesday at Brighton at the age of seventy, was a learned Biblical and Oriental scholar and writer. For the British Museum, where he was in charge of the Hebrew, Syriac and Ethiopia MSS from 1891 till his retirement in 1914, he did much useful work. This included a descriptive list of the Hebrew and Samaritan MSS in the Museum, published in 1893. To this he added a catalogue of these MSS, which appeared in three volumes at intervals between 1899 and 1915. In 1899, also, he published a descriptive list of Syriac and Karshuni MSS acquired by the Museum since 1873. His other works were 'The Superlinear Punctuation', 1893, and editions of the Liturgy of the Nile, Palestinian Syriac and English, 1896, of recently discovered portions of the Palestinian Syriac Version of Holy Scripture, 1896, of Ibn al-Hiti's Arabic Chronicle of Karaite Doctors, with an English translation, 1897, and of the original Hebrew of Ecclesiastics XXXI &c., 1899, also 'Hebrew Babylonian Affinities', 1899.

Mr Margoliouth was born of Jewish parents in Russian Poland on 4th December, 1853, and was educated at Dusseldorf and the University of Bonn. He was a nephew of the Revd Moses Margoliouth (1820–1881), vicar of Little Linford, the Hebrew scholar. Having prepared at

Cuddesdon, he was ordained in 1881 to the curacy of St Thomas, Leeds, and afterwards, while a curate at Cambridge, entered Queen's College. He had been naturalised as a British subject in 1887. Though illness prevented him from obtaining honours in the Semitic Languages Tripos, he was bracketed equal for the Tyrwhitt Hebrew scholarship in 1891. During his service at the British Museum, he founded the Text and Translation Society for the publication of Oriental Works, and served as its hon. secretary for three years; he was also for three years a member of the Aristotelian Society. On many occasions he examined in Hebrew and Aramaic for the University of London, and was a member of the University Board of Studies in Theology. He contributed articles to the Jewish Quarterly Review and other reviews and maintained an interest in general literature. He married in 1886, Marion, daughter of John Fearon, of Cockermouth.

*

George Margoliouth's address at the time of his death was 4 Albany Villas, Hove, Sussex. In Venn's *Alumni Cantabrigiensis*, he has the following entry: 'Margoliouth, (formerly Epstein). The Revd George, s. of Herschel Epstein, b. 1852. Adopted the name Margoliouth, June, 1878.' This entry in the Cambridge University Library's copy has been interestingly amended by his son: 'B. 4th December, 1853. For *adopted*… 1878, read *reverted* to the name Margoliouth, April, 1878 on being baptised by his paternal uncle the Revd Moses Margoliouth, Vicar of Little Linford, Bucks.' This is perhaps some evidence that Margoliouth was an ancestral name of which the family was proud. He does not correct his grandfather's name. George's son was also, in the family tradition, a distinguished scholar. Herschel Maurice (or Moses) Margoliouth was born in 1887. Moses' widow, who died two years later, left one hundred pounds for the education of the child. He attended Rugby School where he became head boy, and first attended Oriel College, Oxford, in 1906. After a short spell of teaching at Marlborough, he served with distinction in the First World War, achieving the rank of captain. He occupied several academic posts, eventually, in 1935, becoming a Fellow of Oriel. He was an acknowledged expert on 17th to 19th century English poetry, and himself published a book of poems in 1948: *Intimation and Other Poems*. Herschel Margoliouth died 20th March, 1959.

Appendix VI
Ezekiel Margoliouth

London missionary to the Jews. Came from Suwalki. Friend of Moses Margoliouth but not related to him (unless very remotely).

Ezekiel Margoliouth was born in 1816 in Suwalki, the son of the chief Rabbi there, Abraham Margoliouth. He had three daughters, Hannah, Mary and Elizabeth, and a son, David Samuel (see below). His wife's name was Sarah. Ezekiel was baptised in 1848 and then worked for the rest of his life for the CMJ. He died in 1894.

His daughter Mary married Michael Rosenthal, a missionary to the Jews and the son of a Rabbi, on 28th October, 1874 (a fortnight after Moses' second marriage). Interestingly, and possibly through Moses' influence, Michael Rosenthal was appointed curate at St Paul's, Haggerston, serving under Revd S.J. Stone. Ezekiel's daughter Elizabeth, went to stay with Moses' widow in Little Linford for a short time after Moses' death, showing that the two families enjoyed close ties of friendship. In 'Some Jewish Witnesses for Christ,' by Revd A. Bernstein (1909), Ezekiel is described as 'an Hebraist equal to any of his day.' Bernstein also says, 'He had a profound knowledge of the Talmud, rare even amongst Talmudists. It was, however, in the composition of modern Hebrew that his chief talent lay. His father, Abraham, had been thirty-three years a chief Rabbi, and his mother could trace twelve

Rabbis amongst her ancestors. At the age of twenty-seven he confessed faith in Christ as his Saviour, though his wife, whom he had married the previous year, for a long time refused to become a Christian. He then came over to England, where she afterwards joined him, and in 1848 also became a Christian. He studied to learn bookbinding. In 1852 he was appointed a missionary of the LJS (later CMJ) in London, and worked as such almost to the end of his life. His son is the Revd Professor David S. Margoliouth, D. Lit., Laudian Professor of Arabic at Oxford University, and Examining Chaplain to the Bishop of Liverpool.'

David Samuel Margoliouth was born in 1858. He was educated at New College, Oxford, obtaining M.S. and D. Lit. degrees. From 1881 to 1889 he held a fellowship in Arabic at New College. In 1896 he married Jessie (d. 1933), daughter of R. Payne Smith, Dean of Canterbury. He was appointed Laudian professor of Arabic in 1889, and continued in that post until his retirement in 1937. He was ordained by the Bishop of Oxford on 7th February, 1900. He was moderator in oriental languages and Hibbert lecturer in oriental history at the University of Punjab, a reader in Arabic history at the University of Calcutta; and Wilson lecturer at Bombay University in 1929. He was one of the outstanding orientalists of his day, and was frequently honoured by learned societies. In 1929 he represented the British Government at the Orientalist Conference in Athens. In 1931 he was president of the John Payne Society. He wrote numerous books. He latterly lived in Oxford, and died in 1940.

Moses Margoliouth
Published Works

The Fundamental Principles of Modern Judaism Investigated (including Memoir and Preface by Henry Raikes), London, 1843

Israel's Ordnances Examined, London, 1844

The Star of Jacob (periodical), edited by M.M. nos 1–6, Dublin, 1847

A Pilgrimage to the Land of My Fathers, London, Bentley, 1850, 8vo, 2 vols

The History of the Jews in Great Britain, London, 1851, 3 vols, 12vo

Genuine Freemasonry Indissolubly Connected with Revelation, London, 1852

Vestiges of Genuine Freemasonry Amongst the Ruins of Asia & c., Manchester, 1852

Holmfirth's Solemn Voice (sermon on the Holmfirth disaster), London, 1852

The Apostolic Triple Benediction (sermon), Manchester, 1853

Genuine Repentance and its Effect: An exposition of the Fourteenth Chapter of Hosea, London, 1854, 8vo

Farewell Address to the Parishioners of Wybunbury, Manchester, 1855, 12vo

The Lord's Anointed (sermon preached in Moscow), London, 1856 (second edition, London, 1874)

The Anglo-Hebrews: Their Past Wrongs and Present Grievances, London, Booth, 1856, 8vo

The Quarrel of God's Covenant (a fast day sermon), London 1857

The Curates of Riversdale, 1860, 3 vols

What is Man? (sermon), Oxford, 1860

Sacred Minstrelsy: A Lecture on Biblical and Post-Biblical Hebrew Music, London, 1860

The Gospel and its Mission (sermon), London, 1860

The End of the Law (two sermons with other notes), London 1861

England's Crown of Rejoicing (a sermon preached on the Sunday before the marriage of Albert Edward, Prince of Wales), London, 1863

The Spirit of Prophecy (four sermons), London, 1864

The Haidad: A Harvest Thanksgiving sermon, London, 1864

Abyssinia: Its Past, Present and Probable Future, London, 1866, 8 vols

Professor Selwyn's Latin Thanks (in Hebrew verse), London, 1867

The Oracles of God and their Vindication (sermon), London, 1870

Vestiges of the Historic Anglo-Hebrews in East Anglia, London, 1870, 8 vols

The Poetry of the Hebrew Pentateuch (four essays), London 1871

The Bane of a Parasite Ritual (sermon), London, 1872

The Lord's Prayer, no adaptation of Existing Jewish Petitions, explained by the Light of 'The Day of the Lord' in a series of six essays, plus two more, London, 1876, 8 vols

An Exposition of the 53rd Chapter of Isaiah (sermon)

The Destinies of Israel and the Claims of Hebrew Christians upon Sitting Congress, 1878

Some Triumphs and Trophies of the Light of the World, London, 1882, 8 vols (as in list of British Library, 1998)

Index

MOSES

A SHORT ACCOUNT OF THE LIFE OF
REVEREND MOSES MARGOLIOUTH

Moses Margoliouth was born and raised in Suwalki,
an impoverished town in the north-east of Poland.
Stifled by the rigid structure of his Jewish
upbringing, he fled his homeland in 1837 and
settled in the cosmopolitan port of Liverpool. He
fell in love with the great institutions of British
heritage and became a Christian convert. He went
on to excel as a Hebraic scholar at Trinity College
Dublin and, on his return to Liverpool, was
ordained into the Church of England.

As Peter Jones carefully excavates the diverse
fragments of Moses' life, we begin to appreciate the
extraordinary drive of this man and the influence he
had on his contemporaries. A seemingly tireless
imbiber of life and a devout Christian who
nevertheless retained pride in his Jewish roots, he
scattered himself and his convictions about Europe
and the near East. His heart, however, remained in
England, the place of his conversion.

COVER PHOTOGRAPH: carved head of the
Empress Lucilla, Consort of Lucius Verus, 160 AD,
discovered 10 Aug 1847.

RIGHT: Drawing of Reverend Moses Margoliouth
with the carved head of Empress Lucilla by Lewis
Ferriere, British vice-consul at Tunis.

UK £8.99

ISBN 0-75410-728-0

9 780754 107286

www.minerva-press.co.uk